# Law & Lawyers on

## An essential guide and resource for legal practitioners

# Internet Handbooks

*Other titles in preparation*

# Law
# & Lawyers
## on the internet

An essential guide and resource for
legal practitioners

Stephen Hardy
&
Michael Base

www.internet-handbooks.co.uk

Other titles by Dr Stephen Hardy

*The English Legal System* (Studymates)
*Studying Law on the Internet* (Internet Handbooks)

Dedication – To UCL friends past (1989–93) and present.

First published in 2001 by Internet Handbooks Ltd, Plymbridge House, Estover Road, Plymouth PL6 7PY, United Kingdom.

| Customer services tel: | (01752) 202301 |
| --- | --- |
| Orders fax: | (01752) 202333 |
| Customer services email: | cservs@plymbridge.com |
| Distributors web site: | www.plymbridge.com |
| Internet Handbooks web site: | www.internet-handbooks.co.uk |

Typeset by PDQ Typesetting, Newcastle-under-Lyme.
Printed and bound by The Cromwell Press Ltd, Trowbridge, Wiltshire.

# Contents

. . . . . . . . . . . . . . . . . . . . . . . . . . . . . . . . . . . . . . . . . . . . . . . . . . .

# Contents ................................................

# List of illustrations

. . . . . . . . . . . . . . . . . . . . . . . . . . . . . . . . . . . . . . . . . . . . . . . . . . . . . . . . . . . . . .

# Preface

With the expansion of technology in both legal practice and learning, to ignore the internet as a legal resource would be a great mistake. With more than 100,000 legal practitioners across the UK, it is hoped that this guide to the salient legal web sites and electronic legal information should prove a valuable resource for practitioners whether web literate or not.

The terms email, ecommerce and the web are becoming much more familiar today, and their applications in the legal world are growing fast. This offers a particular challenge to law which has so long been steeped in medieval tradition. However, legal education is rapidly embracing the information revolution, and legal services and law providers everywhere are gearing themselves up for change. The thousands of UK and other law web sites, and the Lord Chancellor's Advisory Group on IT, are clear evidence of these changes. Just as business today demands a strong net presence, so too does law.

Lawyers often think that they are the last to feel the impact of the revolution in technology. This is true since most lawyers have got their collective heads around email, if only to send silly jokes to their friends. However, as this guide will demonstrate, the smart money has already welcomed the new trend. In augmenting their traditional client-based advisory work, some firms now reach further and further into clients' systems, data and business processes, checking protocols and legality, with most of the workforce oblivious to their presence. In doing so they gain greater and more stable revenue, and create an almost unbreakable client relationship. In addition, many services hitherto dismissed as un-economic have now reappeared in electronic form, further bolstering the competitive advantage of those embracing change. The truth is that we do not have a 'technological' revolution, but a revolution in the creation, presentation and delivery of facts, opinions and information, the bedrock of the law. So, to ignore the further reaches of cyberspace is not only a great mistake but a mistake which will put law firms at a considerable disadvantage. How these trends will continue is still conjecture. If what we have found in the writing of this guide is the beginning, then it will happen faster, bring greater change and result in more corporate blood-letting than you think.

The aim of this handbook is to present a comprehensive and conveni-ent set of web site reviews of the key law associations, legal information and services providers, as well as European and national legal institutions, and advice on how to efficiently access these systems. Part One aims to show lawyers how to use the internet as a legal resource, and introduces the major online legal institutions, legal information points and law asso-ciations. Part Two reviews relevant law sites pertinent to a wide range of professional legal practice. It is hoped the guide will help you prepare ef-fectively for the rapidly emerging world of ecommerce and e-law.

We pay tribute to the many lawyers and law firms, and others, for creating so many excellent web sites to review. If a particular site has been missed, please accept our apologies. We would be delighted to receive details of that, or of any other new services which could usefully be mentioned in a subsequent edition of this book.

*Stephen Hardy & Michael Base*
*hardybase@internet-handbooks.co.uk*

# 1 Introducing law on the internet

**In this chapter we will explore:**

▶ *the digital revolution*
▶ *what is the internet?*
▶ *legal training online*
▶ *some law web sites to sample*
▶ *internet tutorials for lawyers*

. . . . . . . . . . . . . . . . . . . . . . . . . . . . . . . . . . . . . . . . . . . . . . . . . . . . . . . . .

## The digital revolution

In the last couple of years, a huge number of new law sites and services has been launched onto the internet. But what are they like? What are the new services being developed by professional lawyers, by government and judicial departments, and by internet companies? What impact is the internet likely to have on the delivery of legal and judicial services, on the operation of the courts, and the careers of those working in the legal profession?

The digital and internet revolution is gathering momentum, and the legal profession is now beginning to embrace it strongly. Already many lawyers have their own web sites offering their professional services, and the courts have seen the widespread introduction of computer technology to assist them.

## What is the internet?

The world 'internet' is a broad term which refers to the fast-expanding network of global computers that can access each other in seconds by phone and satellite links. If you are using a modem on your computer, you too are part of the internet. The general term 'internet' encompasses a variety of elements:

1.  Email – the sending and receiving of electronic mail and files (such as word processed documents).

2.  The world wide web (the 'web') – a vast network of web sites consisting of individual web pages.

3.  Internet chat – using technology such as internet relay chat (IRC) or ICQ ('I Seek You') to exchange typed messages with other internet chatters in real time, in a public or private chatroom.

4.  Newsgroups – The 80,000-plus newsgroups are collectively referred to as Usenet, and millions of people use them every day. To read and post messages in newsgroups you need some newsreading software, typically Outlook Express or Netscape Messenger. The ever-growing newsgroups have been around for much longer than the world wide web, and are an endless source of distributed information, gossip, news, entertainment, sex, politics, resources and ideas.

5. Internet mailing lists – sometimes called emailing lists. You can sub-scribe to these for free, getting the messages regularly sent to your email address, and you can post messages for fellow list members to read. There are around 90,000 of these lists covering every topic under the sun.

6. Bulletin board services (BBS) – a kind of notice board system for posting messages.

7. Video conferencing – using software such as Windows NetMeeting to communicate audio-visually with other people in real time.

8. Telnet – software that allows you to connect across the internet to a remote computer (e.g. a university department or library). You can then access that computer as if you were on a local terminal linked to that system.

9. File transfer protocol (FTP) – the method the internet uses to speed files back and forth between computers. In practice you don't need to worry about FTP unless you are thinking about creating and pub-lishing your own web pages: then you would need some of the freely available FTP software to upload your pages to your web hosting ser-vice.

Speaking of 'the internet' can be compared with the way we speak of 'the printed word' when we mean books, magazines, newspapers, newslet-ters, catalogues, leaflets, tickets and posters. To most people 'the internet' means email, and web pages.

*A major cultural revolution*
People have compared the internet and digital revolution with the birth of book printing technology, developed by Joseph Gutenberg, William Caxton and others in Europe in the 1500s. As we all know, the arrival of book printing had a massive impact on society then, and has done ever since.

Email has been around for 20 years or more, but the world wide web has only been around since 1994, and is still in a very early stage of devel-opment. We are witnessing the very beginning of an enormous revolution in global digital communications, one which is likely to have a massive impact on how future generations live and work.

## Legal training online

Many legal training services have begun to go online. For examples, see:

http://www.plcinfo.com

http://www.2ends.com

http://itlaw.law.strath.ac.uk

Fig. 1. PLC Info is a good example of a practical online legal information service for business lawyers.

Many law schools have decided to create online learning spaces, or to put handouts on web pages. This rapid usage of the internet is a clear sign of the growing importance – and acceptance of – the new medium.

## Some law web sites to sample

Just to give you some ideas on the law and the internet why not sample these test sites:

*The Cyber Law Centre*
http://www.cyberlawcentre.org.uk
According to *Internet Magazine,* 'The Cyber Law Centre is a collection of legal resources, includes relevant links, mailing lists and research tools, with more to come. One of the most interesting elements is the conference, which seems reasonably active, and this whole site is well on the way to developing into a valuable resource for legal beagles.'

*Data Protection Registrar*
http://www.open.gov.uk/dpr/dprhome.htm
This site maintained by the Data Protection Registrar covers the latest regulations concerning the collation, reproduction and access to electronic and other data. Very useful to consider before using the net!

*Internet Law & Policy Forum*
http://www.perkinscoie.com
This is a discussion site run by the Internet Law & Policy Forum. It provides a setting for debates on law governing the internet and the internet's use. This is a very good place to explore some of the latest issues.

# Introducing law on the internet ......................................

*Internet Law Update*
http://www.collegehill.com/ilp-news/
Try this site and view the information it has put together on internet law. The Internet Law Update site gives exactly what its title states, 'an updating' service.

*Society for Computers and Law*
http://www.scl.org
The emergence of the Society for Computers and Law is a clear sign of the times, given the increased importance of law and the internet. It enables a group of like-minded people to exchange information and views.

## Internet tutorials for lawyers

Lastly, if you are still having trouble in using the internet, you could check out the following web sites:

*Internet Tutorials for Lawyers*
http://www.pavilion.co.uk/legal/guide.htm
The Internet Tutorials for Lawyers is accredited for 8 hours under the substantive law and training component of the New Practitioners' Programme. When ordering the Guide, let the Law Society know that you wish to receive accreditation and they will tell you what to do.

Fig. 2. Internet Tutorial.

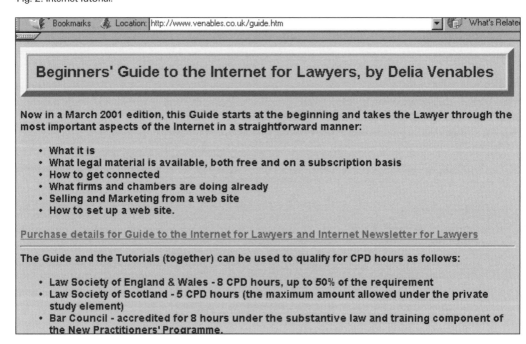

Bookmarks   Location: http://www.venables.co.uk/guide.htm   What's Related

## Beginners' Guide to the Internet for Lawyers, by Delia Venables

Now in a March 2001 edition, this Guide starts at the beginning and takes the Lawyer through the most important aspects of the Internet in a straightforward manner:

- What it is
- What legal material is available, both free and on a subscription basis
- How to get connected
- What firms and chambers are doing already
- Selling and Marketing from a web site
- How to set up a web site.

Purchase details for Guide to the Internet for Lawyers and Internet Newsletter for Lawyers

The Guide and the Tutorials (together) can be used to qualify for CPD hours as follows:

- Law Society of England & Wales - 8 CPD hours, up to 50% of the requirement
- Law Society of Scotland - 5 CPD hours (the maximum amount allowed under the private study element)
- Bar Council - accredited for 8 hours under the substantive law and training component of the New Practitioners' Programme.

Now that you have tried these sites, in the following chapters we will present law sites for you to explore and utilise in your legal research, practice and networking with other lawyers. We will start by exploring online legal institutions, electronic law reporting, and law associations on the net. In Part Two (Electronic legal resources) we present specialist chapters covering the major areas of legal practice. In addition of these primary aims, we hope to give guidance to new net users on where to find law, to give confidence to legal advisors in using the web as a research tool, and to give some tips on key legal 'link' sites.

## Problems with web site addresses

In case you experience a problem accessing a particular web page, here are some tips to help you. First, check that you have entered the URL correctly. Next, try to access the site again later, as even the best sites may be overwhelmed with traffic, or temporarily closed for maintenance. If that doesn't work, strip the URL back to its root address (in case the site's individual web pages have been reorganised) and try again. For example:

http://www.sitename.com/folder/page.html
http://www.sitename.com

Finally, the site may have moved to a new URL, without leaving a forwarding link. If so, try using one of the excellent search engines mentioned in the appendix of this book. If that fails too, the site may for some reason have been withdrawn from service. In this case the search engine may suggest some useful alternatives.

## Some more Internet Handbooks to help you

▶ *Education & Training on the Internet* by Laurel Alexander. An essential reference source for students, teachers, and education providers.

▶ *Getting Connected to the Internet* by Ian Hosker. A practical step-by-step guide to going online for the very first time.

▶ *Getting Started on the Internet* by Kye Valongo. A practical step-by-step guide to email, browsing, searching and other aspects of using the internet.

A free illustrated catalogue is available from the publishers (see back cover for details).

# 2 Online legal institutions and links

**In this chapter we will explore:**

▶ *UK legal institutions online*
▶ *UK government web sites*
▶ *the courts*
▶ *law links, portals and gateways*

## UK legal institutions online

*Lord Chancellor's Department*
http://www.open.gov.uk/lcd/lcdhome.htm
This 'gateway' site from the Lord Chancellor's Department (LCD) explains the main departmental role of the Lord Chancellor. It covers the management of the courts, the appointment of judges and magistrates, and the administration of legal aid, recent government legislation and reform. In particular, the What's New?, press notices and speeches services give up-to-date information about the latest state of the law. Moreover, the LCD Research site gives information on pending law reform and current recent projects. The remainder of this 'gateway' site is divided into three areas:

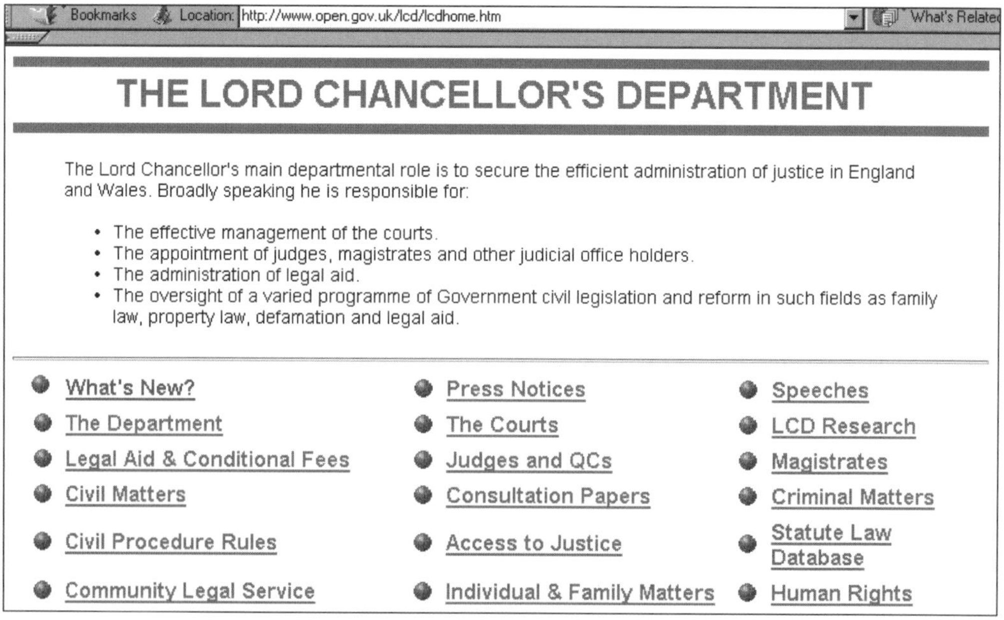

Fig. 3. The web site of the Lord Chancellor's Department is an essential bookmark for lawyers using the internet.

1. Subject legal information, divided into the civil and criminal jurisdictions.

2. Statute law and human rights databases.

Bookmarks    Location: http://www.open.gov.uk/lcd/lcdhome.htm     What's Related

# THE LORD CHANCELLOR'S DEPARTMENT

The Lord Chancellor's main departmental role is to secure the efficient administration of justice in England and Wales. Broadly speaking he is responsible for:

- The effective management of the courts.
- The appointment of judges, magistrates and other judicial office holders.
- The administration of legal aid.
- The oversight of a varied programme of Government civil legislation and reform in such fields as family law, property law, defamation and legal aid.

| | | |
|---|---|---|
| ● What's New? | ● Press Notices | ● Speeches |
| ● The Department | ● The Courts | ● LCD Research |
| ● Legal Aid & Conditional Fees | ● Judges and QCs | ● Magistrates |
| ● Civil Matters | ● Consultation Papers | ● Criminal Matters |
| ● Civil Procedure Rules | ● Access to Justice | ● Statute Law Database |
| ● Community Legal Service | ● Individual & Family Matters | ● Human Rights |

3. The invaluable 'related links' area. This gives access to other Government departments and agencies, legislative sources (e.g. Parliament, HMSO, Inquiries, and other useful sites such as the Bar Council, Law Society and others). The latter function gives rise to the title of 'gateway' site or 'portal', since accessing this site gives you quick access to over fifty other law and law-related sites.

*UK Government*
http://www.open.gov.uk
This is the UK Government's primary web site. This service provides an accessible entry point to information on the UK public sector. It has both organisation and topic indices, as well as a quick search tool. From this other gateway site you can access:

Government departments
Parliament
Public Inquiries
Royal Commissions
Local authorities
Other public services providers

Its useful What's New page gives some valuable insights into the latest new sites available on the world wide web.

*House of Lords' Judicial Business*
http://www.parliament.the-station.pa/ld199697/ldjudgmnt
This is the House of Lords' Judicial Business site. It contains full transcripts of the judgments delivered by the UK's highest court since 14 November 1996. Furthermore, it provides details of where to obtain paper copies of House of Lords judgments. Easily accessible, this site is an efficient research tool.

*Europa*
http://www.europa.eu.int
This European site can be read in eleven different working languages of the European Union. It gives you access to the major institutions of the EU, including:

The Council
The European Parliament
The European Commission
The European Court of Justice (ECJ)

Each institution provides information on the latest EU regulations, policies, and proposed legislative changes. The ECJ site provides access to its case law since 1964 (see: www.europa.eu.int/cj), and directly connects to the ECJ's database and researching facilities.

Apart from these key gateway sites, the Government has directed that its departments be accessible to the public. Below are some of its main departments with web sites:

# Online legal institutions and links.....................................

## UK government web sites

*Central Office of Information*
http://www.coi.gov.uk/coi/depts/deptlist.html
The Central Office of Information provides an archive of all the government's press releases, organised by department and by date.

*Court Service*
http://www.courtservice.gov.uk
The Court Service is an executive agency of the Lord Chancellor's Department. It supplies administrative support to a number of courts and tribunals across England and Wales. These include the High Court, the Crown Court and the county courts. Its prime aim is to promote an impartial and efficient operation. While the outcome of cases coming before these courts and tribunals is determined by a judge or a judicial officer, much of the supporting administrative work is carried out by Court Service staff.

Fig. 4. The UK Court Service.

   The Court Service web site provides a 'map' of the overall court system indicating, in red type, where judgments are already available on the site. This site allows lawyers access to all the higher courts within the UK from the comfort of your own desk.

*Criminal Justice System*
http://www.criminal-justice-system.gov.uk
This UK government web site is a good source of links to the various criminal justice departments online, and to a selection of publications.

*Government Information Service*
http://www.open.gov.uk/index.htm
This organisation provides links to many government departments and organisations, including regulatory bodies. There is a search engine relating to all UK government servers (including local government) and a What's New section containing government press releases.

*Health & Safety Executive*
http://www.open.gov.uk/hse/hsehome.htm
The Health & Safety Executive's (HSE) site provides information on health and safety laws and regulations, statistical data, and information on the responsibilities and work of its inspectorate.

*Home Office*
http://www.homeoffice.gov.uk
The site says: 'The Home Office is the government department responsible for internal affairs in England and Wales. The principal aim of the Home Office is to build a safe, just and tolerant society in which the rights and responsibilities of individuals, families and communities are properly balanced and the protection and security of the public are maintained.' This online service is a source of press releases, research data, publications and legislation. These cover the fields of:

    Constitutional and community issues
    Human rights
    Race equality
    Freedom, of information
    Data protection
    Elections
    Political parties
    European issues
    Criminal justice

*Inland Revenue*
http://www.inlandrevenue.gov.uk
The Inland Revenue is responsible, under the overall direction of Treasury Ministers, for the efficient administration of income tax, tax credits, corporation tax, capital gains tax, petroleum revenue tax, inheritance tax, national insurance contributions, and stamp duties. The Inland Revenue's site gives details of the UK's current fiscal arrangements and laws.

*Law Commission for England and Wales*
http://www.lawcom.gov.uk/misc/about.htm
http://www.open.gov.uk/lawcomm
The Law Commission is the independent body set up by Parliament in 1965 (along with a similar Commission for Scotland) to keep the law of England and Wales under review and to recommend reform when it is needed. At any one time the Commission is engaged on between 20 and 30 projects of law reform, at different stages of completion. A typical project will begin with a study of the area of law in question, and an

attempt to identify its defects. Foreign systems of law will be examined to see how they deal with similar problems. The Law Commission's site gives details of the latest and archive law reform papers and consultation documents available. It also has details of its latest research programmes.

*Legal Aid*
http://www.legalservices.gov.uk
Publicly-funded legal services in England and Wales are now administered by the Legal Services Commission (LSC). See below.

*Official Solicitor*
http://www.offsol.demon.co.uk
The Office of Official Solicitor provides representation for persons under legal disability, and others, in county court or High Court proceedings in England and Wales. This site gives both technical and practical information for the legal profession, and for members of the general public. There are links to the legal basis of the office, other resources, child abduction, find a solicitor, full contents, and solicitors on the web. The site includes a large number of Practice Directions and Notes.

*Public Record Office*
http://www.pro.gov.uk

*Public Trust Office*
http://www.publictrust.gov.uk

*Treasury Solicitor*
http://www.open.gov.uk/tsd/tsdhome.htm

The court system in the UK is both complex and hierarchical. However, the advent of computer technology in court – even if only to print off DVLA documents for road traffic offenders – is a sign of progress. Consequently, the courts are utilising technology more and more. In the next section we look at courts on the web.

## The Courts

*Coroners*
http://www.homeoffice.gov.uk/new_indexs/index_coroner.htm
The Home Office has developed this page of information and links about the work of the Coroners, and some recent high profile cases.

*Court Service*
As noted above, the Court Service's web site offers selected judgments, practice directions, forms and leaflets. See also:

*Court of Appeal (Civil Division)*
http://www.courtservice.gov.uk/notices/civil/not_civil.htm
This is the Court Service's site for the Court of Appeal (Civil Division). It includes a court guide and notices and a review of the legal year.

*Court of Appeal (Criminal Division).*
http:// www.courtservice.gov.uk/crimhome.htm
This is the Court Service's site for the Court of Appeal (Criminal Division).
It includes notices, and a guide to proceedings.

*High Court*
http://www.courtservice.gov.uk/highhome.htm
This is the Court Service's site with links to various services including the:

| | |
|---|---|
| Queen's Bench Division | Admiralty Court |
| Commercial Court | Crown Office |
| Technology & Construction Court | Chancery Division |
| Patents Court | Family Division |

*HM Judges*
http://www.open.gov.uk/lcd/judicial/judgesfr.htm
This site provides information on HM judges – how to apply, who they are, their salaries, and the office. In particular there are links to judicial appointments, current appointment competitions, judicial appointments procedures, general information and annual reports, judicial statistics, guidance on outside activities and interests, a list of the senior judiciary, judicial salary scales, judgments, speeches by senior judges and information about the legal year.

*Legal Aid and the Legal Services Commission*
http://www.open.gov.uk/lab/legal.htm
The Legal Aid site informs people about: who can apply, income limits and how to get it. It is very useful for statistical data. Publicly-funded legal services in England and Wales are now administered by the Legal Services Commission (LSC). Information about the Commission, its

Fig. 5. The Legal Services Commission web site.

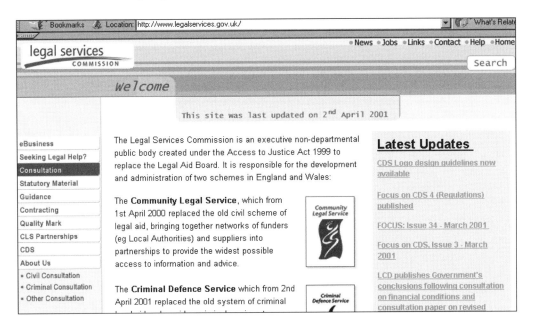

19

work and the current funding scheme can be found on its own web site at:

http://www.legalservices.gov.uk

*Legal Services Commission*
http://www.legalservices.gov.uk
The Legal Services Commission is a new executive non-departmental public body created under the Access to Justice Act 1999. It exists to develop and administer two schemes in England and Wales:

1.  The Community Legal Service. This replaces the old civil scheme of legal aid, bringing together networks of funders (e.g. local authorities) and suppliers into partnerships to provide the widest possible access to information and advice.

2.  The Criminal Defence Service. From April 2001 this has replaced the old system of criminal legal aid and provides criminal services to people accused of crimes. Its web site is a source of statutory material and guidance.

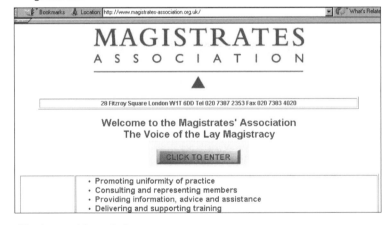

*Magistrates' Association*
http://www.magistrates-association.org.uk
See the entry on page 47.

*Northern Ireland Court Service*
http://www.nics.gov.uk/pubsec/courts/courts.htm
Check out this site for the Courts' charter and various other publications. A number of these are available online in downloadable PDF format.

*Official Solicitor*
http://www.offsol.demon.co.uk
The Office of Official Solicitor provides representation for persons under legal disability (and others) in county court or High Court proceedings in England and Wales. The Official Solicitor is guardian *ad litem* or next friend of last resort. His office can be traced back to medieval times since the state has always recognised need for representation of an incapacitated person when a benevolent relative or friend cannot be found

to act on his behalf. This site gives both technical and practical information for the legal profession, and for members of the general public. Some important changes took effect from 1 April 2001, and information about this is available here

*Royal Courts of Justice Daily Lists*
http://wood.ccta.gov.uk/courtser/dailylist.nsf
The Royal Courts of Justice Daily Lists are to be found here.

*Scottish Court Service*
http://www.scotcourts.gov.uk
This site provides a useful access point to information relating to all civil and criminal courts within Scotland. These include the Court of Session, the High Court of Justiciary, the Sheriff Courts and a number of other courts, commissions and tribunals as well the District Courts. The information includes location details, contact numbers, advice and details of recent significant judgments. The site is regularly updated.

*Scottish Law Commission*
http://www.scotlawcom.gov.uk
The Scottish Law Commission is an independent body established by the Law Commissions Act of 1965. In choosing areas of work the Commission is guided by judges, lawyers, government departments, the Scottish Administration and the general public who provide information of their experiences in applying a particular area of the law or in obtaining legal remedies. The Commission's web site publications page contains the full texts of all discussion papers and reports published since September 2000. This includes its current sixth programme of law reform and its 34th Annual Report which gives an overview of its recent work. You can browse or download any of this material.

In the final part of this chapter, we review some law links and portal sites:

## Law links, portals and gateways

*Access to Law*
http://www.accesstolaw.org/default.asp
This contains a useful collection of both UK and international law links.

*British and Irish Legal Information Institute*
http://www.bailii.org
The site offers comprehensive and searchable access to freely available British and Irish public legal information including cases and legislation. As at October 2000, BAILII included 19 databases covering 5 jurisdictions. The system is said to contain over two gigabytes of legal materials and well over 250,000 searchable documents with about 5.5 million hypertext links.

*Cavendish Law Publishers*
http://www.cavendishpublishing.com/cavmaster.html
Cavendish Law Publishers offers a service to law students and users of

its books. In this site Cavendish has developed a very useful and neatly organised collection of law links to everything from law schools to law reports and legal information for the USA, Asia and elsewhere.

*Cyber Law Centre*
http://www.cyberlawcentre.org.uk/
This is 'the site that cites intellectual property resources on the net.' According to *Internet Magazine*: 'The Cyber Law Centre is a collection of legal resources, includes relevant links, mailing lists and research tools, with more to come. One of the most interesting elements is the conference, which seems reasonably active, and this whole site is well on the way to developing into a valuable resource for legal beagles.' The site is maintained by Hannah Oppenheim, a Member of the Computer Law Association and Association of Internet Users.

*Delia Venables Law Portal*
http://www.venables.co.uk
The Delia Venables portal to UK legal resources is an excellent source of free legal information for individuals and companies. It links to solicitors' and barristers' web sites and a large number of other online legal resources in the UK. You can find out about online services from the legal publishers, and free legal current awareness sources. There are links to legal networks of solicitors and barristers on the web (about 60 chambers or individual barristers so far). You will also find legal sites and resources for many other countries including within Europe, the USA, Canada, Australia and New Zealand, China and Japan, and international collections worldwide. The site also includes details of legal training and courses, exhibitions, conferences, legal software and IT suppliers, legal jobs and appointments, arbitration, alternative dispute resolution, legal news and a great deal more.

Fig. 6. Delia Venables Law Links. This is one of the best portal sites for quick access to UK and other web sites.

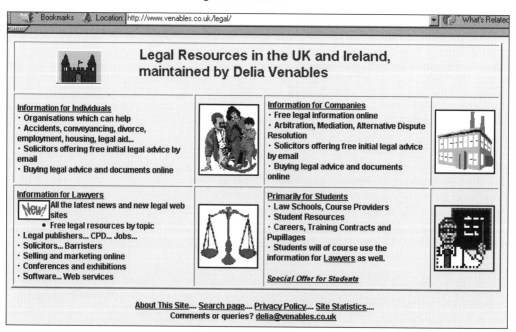

*Findlaw*

http://www.findlaw.com

Launched in 1995, Findlaw is a legal search engine powered by AltaVista. It is a leading international web portal focused on law and government, and provides access to a comprehensive and fast-growing online library of legal resources for use by legal professionals, consumers and small businesses. Its mission is to make legal information on the internet easy to find. A broad array of features includes web search utilities, cases and codes, legal news, mailing lists, message boards and free email. It is very useful as a starting point of access. There are some community boards for discussion of topics such as greedy associates, divorce, employment law, immigration law, copyright law, cyberspace law, and personal injury.

*Infolaw*

http://www.infolaw.co.uk

Infolaw considers legal resources by topic. Arranged A to Z, these include: ADR, arbitration, arts, Australia, aviation, banking, books, building and construction, business and finance, Canada, cases, civil liberties, commercial law generally, companies, computer and communications, conferences and seminars, constitution, consumer, courts, criminal, data bank, data protection, directories, employment, energy, entertainment, environment, equine, Europe, expert witnesses, family, food, forms and precedents, general resources, government, Hong Kong, housing, human rights, immigration, insolvency, insurance, intellectual property, international, internet, Ireland, Jersey, legislation, librarianship, marine, mental health, military, New Zealand, parliament, personal injury, profession, property and conveyancing, Scotland, self help, students and careers, taxation, trade, trusts and estates, welfare and benefits.

Fig. 7. Infolaw.

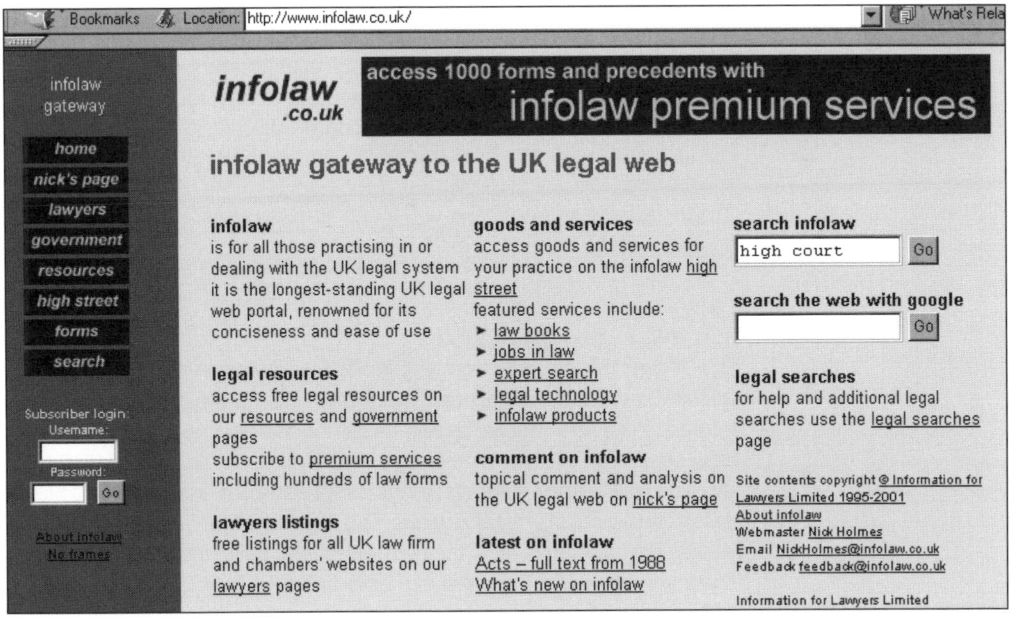

# Online legal institutions and links................................

*Institute of Advanced Legal Study*
http://www.ials.sas.ac.uk
Like the Institute of Advanced Legal Study, Russell Square, London, itself, this law link site provides an online legal library with a wealth of both national and international legal resources.

*JURIST*
http://www.law.cam.ac.uk/jurist
JURIST, the Law Professors' Network, is hosted by Cambridge University's Law Faculty and provides an excellent research tool. It offers research data, including law journals, online articles plus topic and country guides. Online teaching tools including links to UK law schools, and discussion pages for both academics and students. Moreover, it has legal news pages covering both the UK and the world (US Supreme Court, Australian Legal News and others) as well as the latest law reports from the British courts, the International Court, and the European Courts of Justice and Human Rights. As JURIST proclaims, it 'is a clearing house of academically-authored and quality-controlled UK legal resources provided for the convenience of law teachers, law students, lawyers and members of the public in Great Britain and Northern Ireland'.

*Law Links*
http://www.ukc.ac.uk/library/lawlinks/
Law Links is an excellent annotated list of web sites compiled by Sarah Carter at the University of Kent at Canterbury. Well worth a look.

*Law Lounge*
http://www.lawlounge.com/main.htm
This web site consists of a mixed bag of legal links combined with a 'cyber lounge'. Information is classified by topic, such as corporate and commercial, personal and social, criminal, public and administrative, international, information and communication. You can read the latest legal news from Europe, Americas and Australia, and explore a full listing of online academic journals plus links to world general and financial newspapers. Law Lounge bulletin boards discuss a range of topical issues including rights and freedoms, internet law, corporate law and criminal law. The site also features a substantial listing of all the American, British, Australian and Canadian law schools and colleges and law student societies.

*Law Rights*
http://www.lawrights.co.uk/
Law Rights is a privately run and funded company that offers free independent legal information for the public in England and Wales. It was formed to provide concise legal information to both consumers and business customers. It has since expanded to offer a range of direct legal services that use the internet to reduce the time and cost normally associated with seeking legal advice. The legal content on Law Rights is written and updated by a team of barristers, solicitors and academics. There are links to areas dealing with accident claims, adoption, case

examples, consumer topics, employment law, injunctions, children's law, legal aid, private and public housing, relationships, and the Small Claims Court. You can even access Law Rights legal information from your WAP-enabled mobile phone via Law Rights Mobile.

*Law Runner UK*
http://www.ilrg.com/nations/uk
Law Runner UK is a legal search engine, part of larger Internet Legal Resources Guide site.

*LawServe*
http://www.lawserve.co.uk
LawServe is 'the legal internet site run by lawyers, for lawyers.' Information can be found in the following categories: solicitors, expert witnesses, investigators. Solicitors are sorted by the following categories: banking and finance, civil litigation, consumer law, employment, immigration, insolvency, media and entertainment. Details of firms and organisations providing expert witness services can be found for the following specialisations: building and construction, consulting engineers, engineering, handwriting, medical and personal injury.

*Lexicon*
http://www.courtservice.gov.uk/lexicon/index.htm
Lexicon is a web site from the Court Service giving easy access to selected legal information online. It has been designed for the judiciary of England and Wales to be their primary source of online legal information. Its main focus is to provide access to information relevant to the introduction of the Human Rights Act 1998 which came into force in October 2000. The legal links have been structured to give anyone access to legal information on the following areas of law: the United Kingdom, human rights, European and international. The links within each of these areas have been further categorised into current awareness, legislation and treaties, case law, commentary, and organisations. Each link is presented as a descriptive title accompanied by a brief summary to help you determine whether the web site contains the information you are looking for.

*Online Law*
http://www.online-law.co.uk
Online Law is a comprehensive directory providing information on UK law firms, the Inns of Court and Chambers, Barristers, Magistrates courts and expert witnesses.

*UK State*
http://www.ukstate.com
This is a new Stationery Office web-based source of official information. The site provides access to official and legislative information and procedures that are a part of everyday life, covering key life and business events.

# Online legal institutions and links.....................................

Fig. 8. Online Law.

In the next chapter, we find out how to undertake legal research on the internet.

## More Internet Handbooks to help you

▶ *Where to Find it on the Internet* by Kye Valongo (2nd edition). Your complete guide to search engines, portals, databases, yellow pages and other internet reference tools.

A free illustrated catalogue is available from the publishers (see back cover for details).

# 3 The internet for legislation & case law

In this chapter we will explore:

▶ *online law reporting*
▶ *legislation*
▶ *case tracking*
▶ *legal news*
▶ *law journals and legal publications*

. . . . . . . . . . . . . . . . . . . . . . . . . . . . . . . . . . . . . . . . . . . . . . . . . . . . . . . . . . . . . . . . . . . . . . . . . . . . . . .

In this chapter we will consider web sites which will help you to trace case law and find legislation on the internet. As the usage of the web increases, more electronic law reporting is emerging.

## Online law reporting

*Butterworths Law Reporting Service*
http://www.butterworths.co.uk
A chargeable service, the Butterworths Law Reporting Service contains the All England Law Reports and other law reports. A free trial is available.

*Court Service: Judgments*
http://www.courtservice.gov.uk
As mentioned in previous chapters, the Government's Court Service web site contains access to selected Court of Appeal and High Court judgments. The House of Lords dedicated site, referred to in Chapter 2, presents transcripts of Lords decisions since November 1996.

*Sweet & Maxwell Westlaw*
http://www.westlaw.co.uk
Another chargeable service which contains law reports, journals and the latest legal news.

Fig. 9. Butterworths, the law publishers.

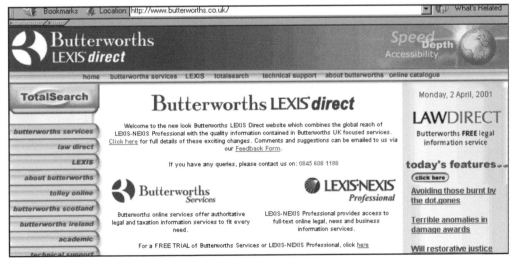

# The internet for legislation & case law ...............................

*European Court of Justice*
http://www.europa.eu.int
This hyperlink site gives access to the ECJ's law reports, as discussed earlier in Chapter 2.

*Incorporated Council of Law Reporters*
http://www.lawreports.co.uk
This site from the Incorporated Council of Law Reporters, the official court reporters, gives you wide-ranging access to all courts' transcripts.

*Masons Law Reports Library*
http://www.masons.com/library/reports/
The City Law Firm, Masons, hosts an online law library site which contains law reports.

*Smith Bernal Law Reports*
http://www.smithbernal.com/casebase_frame.htm
Smith Bernal is a well-known and established law reporting provider, and maintains an online law library. This site also contains a free database of Court of Appeal judgments since April 1996.

Fig. 10. Smith Bernal.

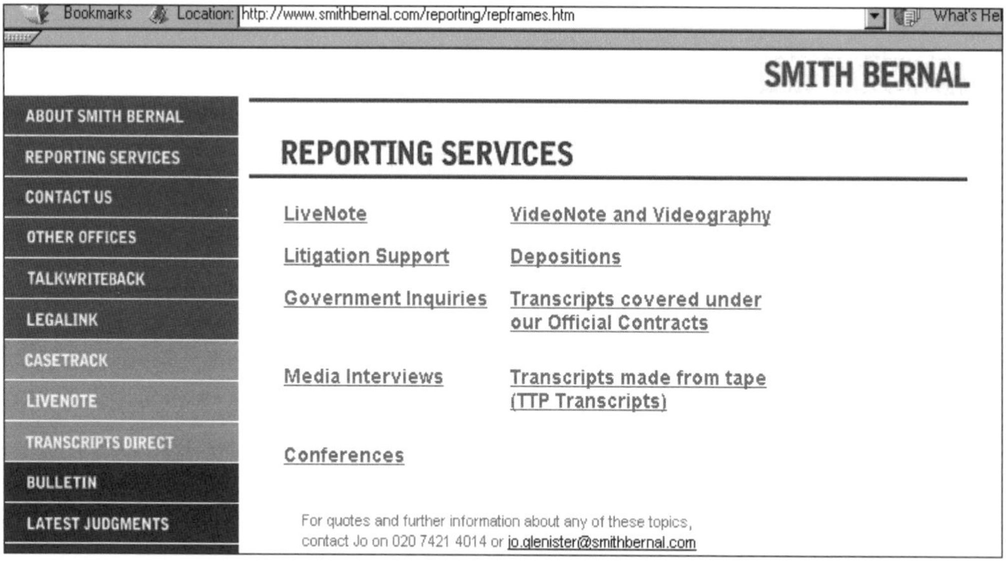

Bookmarks   Location: http://www.smithbernal.com/reporting/repframes.htm    What's He

## SMITH BERNAL

ABOUT SMITH BERNAL

REPORTING SERVICES

CONTACT US

OTHER OFFICES

TALKWRITEBACK

LEGALINK

CASETRACK

LIVENOTE

TRANSCRIPTS DIRECT

BULLETIN

LATEST JUDGMENTS

## REPORTING SERVICES

LiveNote     VideoNote and Videography

Litigation Support     Depositions

Government Inquiries     Transcripts covered under our Official Contracts

Media Interviews     Transcripts made from tape (TTP Transcripts)

Conferences

For quotes and further information about any of these topics, contact Jo on 020 7421 4014 or jo.glenister@smithbernal.com

*Swarbrick Case Index,*
http://chianti.ipl.co.uk/swarb/swarform.html
This site contains the Swarbrick Case Index, a useful tool for finding cases.

*Times Law Reports*
http://www.the-times.co.uk/
This site offers the Times Law Reports, including an archive service.

You can also find some useful journals and legal publications online:

## Legislation

*Butterworths*
http://www.butterworths.co.uk
Butterworths, the well-known law publishers, host a free online legal newspaper. The site also contains a Student Notebook, with student titles, online ordering, case notes, a tour of UK universities, links to other sites and a competition. More importantly for the practitioner are the links to a wide variety of jurisdictions, and various journals. For example:

1. New Law Journal Online – an electronic version of the legal journal.

2. Halsbury's Laws Direct – an online subscription version of Halsbury's Laws of England.

3. All England Direct – includes online subscription access to the All England Law Reports 1936–to date.

4. Law Direct – a current awareness product.

5. The Progress of Legislation database.

6. Practice Directions database supplies full text of all new Practice Directions within a few hours of issue.

7. EC Brief service structured into practice areas and sub-categories.

The Company Search facility provides instant statutory information on all registered UK companies. Users can download images of the latest annual reports, accounts and annual returns as filed at Companies House.

*Westlaw*
http://www.westlaw.co.uk
A comprehensive Sweet & Maxwell legal directory

*Justis*
http://www.justis.com
Context is primarily a publisher of CDs, with the online services intended mainly for updating purposes rather than as separate online services. However, for completeness, here are some of the main CD services:

1. *JUSTIS CELEX* – the full text of all treaties, legislation and judgments of the European Court of Justice.

2. *Electronic Law Reports* – 130 years of *The Law Reports* on two CD ROMs.

3. *JUSTIS Weekly Law* – the full archive of *The Weekly Law Reports* from 1953.

4. *Lloyds Electronic Law Reports* – commercial, maritime, insurance and reinsurance case law from 1919.

5. *The Common Market Law Reports* – the full text of European Community law reports from 1962. Updated five days a week.

*The Stationery Office: Acts Of Parliament*
http://www.hmso.gov.uk/acts.htm
The Stationery Office, formerly the HMSO, the Queen's Official Publishers, publishes on its site full text of Acts as enacted from January 1996. This site is a very useful starting point for tracing the latest version of Acts. Also, this site has a list of the Bills before Parliament, another useful means of monitoring future legal changes.

*The Stationery Office: Statutory Instruments*
http://www.hmso.gov.uk/stat.htm
As with the above-mentioned site for Acts, this site conveniently only covers the increasing number of Statutory Instruments, providing their full texts from 1997.

## Case tracking

*Lawtel*
http://www.lawtel.co.uk
Lawtel, the long established provider of online legal services has offered, by way of subscription unlimited access to all the databases described below, excluding company searches, full text document delivery and new research bureau questions. The subscription services available are:

1. Daily Update – a current awareness service with summaries on all legal developments every 24 hours. There are several ways in which this can be received: (i) a full daily update in all areas of law, (ii) personal daily updates customised to focus on any number of specialities, (iii) an

Fig. 11. Lawtel case reports.

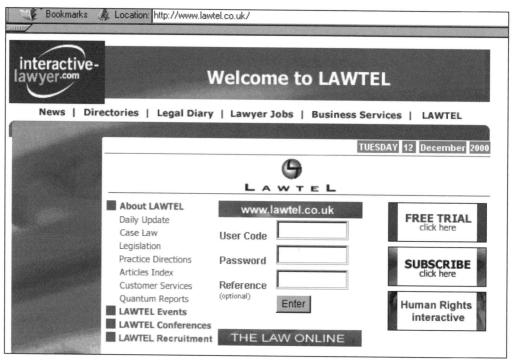

email service with full or personal updates, emailed to as many individuals within a law firm as required, and (iv) an online daily update service consisting of full or customised updates, generated online daily.

2.  Case Law – cases available within 24 hours of judgment being given. Sources include: House of Lords, Privy Council, Court of Appeal, High Court, QBD: Commercial/Admiralty/ Official Referees/Divisional Court/Chancery Division/Family Division; Inferior Courts & Tribunals including: Employment Appeal Tribunal, VAT and Duties Tribunal, Lands Tribunal. Lawtel adds the appropriate reference if a case is subsequently reported elsewhere, e.g. TLR, AER, WLR. It also covers hundreds of unreported cases each month.

3.  Any official judgment from any court, plus advance ordering service; a new tracking service: locates any transcript; personal injury (including quantum); legislation: commencements, repeals, and amendments; statutory instruments; statutes; Parliamentary Bills; Green and White Papers.

4.  European Law – an online service for every EU document published since 1987. It offers full text delivery of any official legal document produced by the Communities since 1953.

5.  Articles Index (25 major and specialist journals) with hypertext links to relevant cases and legislation.

*Lexis-Nexis*
http://www.lexis-nexis.co.uk
Most practitioners will recall Lexis. For many years it was unrivalled in its electronic legal retrieval systems. Some would say it was the forerunner to the world wide web for law. Now modernised and updated, it provides daily free news and updates on:

1.  The European Court of Human Rights.
2.  The European Monetary Union.
3.  European Investment News.

Its non-US legal databases are not yet available in the UK through the internet, although this will come. Subscribers wishing to access the large collections of full text primary source legal materials must in the meantime use the special online service (i.e. not on the web as such). News and business products via the web are already available. These include:

(a) European reQUESTer – a search service for news sources on companies, products, markets, competitors and people.

(b) Tracker – a service to deliver daily targeted information directly to the professional's desktop.

(c) Infotailor – a personal daily briefing service consisting of news and information.

(d) Tell Me More – a service which connects your web site to selected articles from the Lexis-Nexis services. These articles can then be retrieved by your clients who want to know more about a particular topic. Free trials are available.

*Smith Bernal*
http://www.smithbernal.com
Smith Bernal, official reporter to the Courts of Appeal, has recently launched two internet services: Casebase, which is free and Casetrack, which is a subscription service.

1. Casebase is an archive of Court of Appeal and Crown Office cases from April 1996 to '30 days ago'. Full texts of all Court of Appeal and Crown Office cases can be viewed or printed as required. There is an archive comprising more than 20,000 judgments. New judgments are added 30 days after approval, and 600 or more cases are added each month. Transcripts are searchable on case name; date of judgment; case number; and court texts are for personal use only – they may not be used, sold or passed on for commercial gain.

2. Casetrack – is a subscription-based listing, tracking, alerting and full text transcript service for all Court of Appeal and Crown Office cases. Key details of all Court of Appeal and Crown Office cases are listed. Core information is provided about each judgment on the day of judgment. Each case classified is according to key subject area. Each judgment is classified and searchable by name, date, court, court from which the case has been appealed, judge, subject and counsel. Full texts of transcripts are attached as soon as the approved judgment becomes available. There is unlimited access to view, print and download any transcript as required. Full classification of all judgments started in January 1998. Archived cases from April 1996 will also be accessible through the Casetrack service

## Legal news

*Law Society's Gazette*
http://www.lawgazette.co.uk
This site presents the Law Society's Gazette, online.

*The Lawyer Magazine*
http://www.the-lawyer.co.uk
The Lawyer magazine online provides the entire content of each weekly issue. It also ahs search facilities will find stories or features over the last three years. Legal vacancies are also offered for those practitioners looking for employment opportunities.

*International Centre for Commercial Law*
http://www.icclaw.com
Legalease – the International Centre for Commercial Law and IT+Communications – was the first legal publisher to offer online services, first

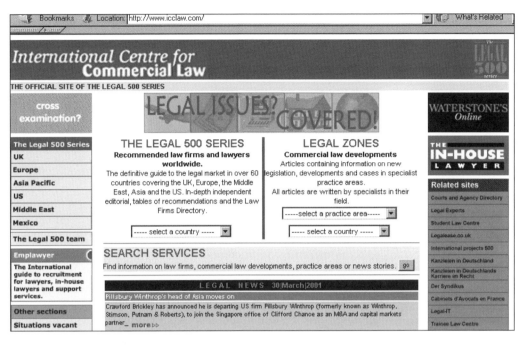

of all (several years ago) with LINK and subsequently with the International Centre for Commercial law. This is one of the largest and most comprehensive legal sites in Europe with over 60,000 pages. It is said to receive 100,000 or more hits each week. In a new venture, there is now also a subscription service for IT and Communications Law.

Fig. 12. ICC Law contains a vast amount of information about law practices and their key personnel.

1. The Legal 500 – It also contains the Legal 500 series of publications, designed as a guide to the top commercial law firms in the UK, Europe and Asia. This includes information on law firms and lawyers in over 60 jurisdictions worldwide, with contact details, specialisations and recommendations.

2. Commercial law developments – There is information on commercial law developments, with contributions from some of Europe's leading law firms. The updates cover a wide variety of subject areas and are designed to provide a regular legal information service to users of the site. The Courts & Agency Directory is perhaps the most comprehensive guide to law firms undertaking agency work in the UK.

3. The Student Law Centre – This includes a free search facility that enables law students to find details of both law firms offering training contracts and barristers chambers offering pupillages, using criteria such as region, work area and start year. A free extensive editorial section has been produced in collaboration with a range of law firms and drawing on the resources and experience of *Legal Business* magazine. There is free advice about preparing a curriculum vitae, interview techniques and timetables for qualifying as either a solicitor or barrister. There are free topical legal updates, and a behind the scenes look

at training at a range of different size law firms and barristers chambers.

4. Subscription services – *IT+Communications Law Journal* (ITCLJ) is a comprehensive source of information on how the law is coping with the digital revolution. Published quarterly, ITCLJ comes in four parts: (a) The Law Reports in a bound volume, (b) a newsletter which provides a summary of each case and its significance, (c) a free computer disk containing all the law reports in WP format (both UK and any relevant foreign cases are included), and (d) the internet site to whcih all subscribers have access, via a unique password, to a private website from which all the law reports can be downloaded.

## Law journals and legal publications

*Butterworths*
http://www.butterworths.co.uk/content/nlj
This site offers selected articles from the more recent *New Law Journal*.

*The Solicitor's Journal*
http://www.smlawpub-holborn.co.uk/lawbrief
This site offers the weekly *Solicitor's Journal*, updated by topic.

*Sweet and Maxwell*
http://www.smlawpub.co.uk
This is the main web site of Sweet and Maxwell, another well-established legal publisher, which now incorporates the previous FTLaw & Tax site. The intention is to amalgamate the services but at the moment, there are two sets of buttons – the left-hand set ('Swiss Cottage') being the original S&M services and the right-hand set ('Holborn') being the

Fig. 13. Sweet & Maxwell, the law publishers.

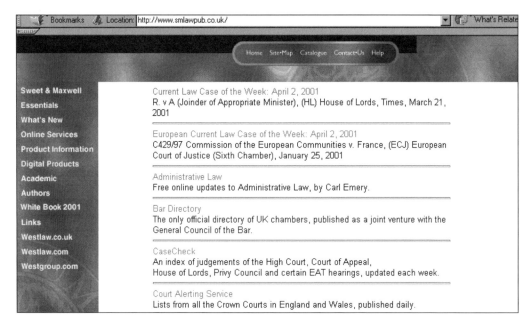

FT&L set. To locate the services below, you have to look partly in the What's New and Internet Services on the left hand side and partly in the Free Online Products on the right. Services include:

1. Badger Alerter – Every day, hundreds of documents are issued from Whitehall, Westminster and the judiciary announcing changes to legislation, new regulations, SIs, decisions, codes of practice and proposals for consultation. This service lists and briefly abstracts every document each day concerning developments of a significant nature, including marked reinforcement or weakening of a legal concept.

2. Law Brief and Case Reports taken from *The Solicitors Journal*. These are grouped under subject headings and list the source of the report.

3. Electronic Newsletters – European Union News Online, Local Government Library. Online, and Planning Bulletin Online.

4. Lists from all the Crown Courts in England and Wales, published daily.

5. Case of the Week – case digests taken from Current Law, European Current Law, and Hong Kong.

6. Student section with 'Inter-Nutcases' – various case digests of special interest to students.

7. The Bar Directory – published with the General Council of the Bar.

8. Kimes International Law Directory – covers 650 law firms in 270 jurisdictions.

9. Online updates are available to *Internet Law and Regulation*, edited by Graham Smith of Bird & Bird, and *Year 2000: Law and Liability* by Susan Singleton.

10. Catalogue of publications, with an online ordering facility.

Subscription services:

1. Current Legal Information – A range of indexes to legal information, providing an easily searchable source of reference to cases, statutes, statutory instruments, articles from legal and financial journals, 'grey paper', official publications and press comment. The service is available on annual subscription in two combinations of database.

2. Current Law Cases – A digest of cases reported since 1986. It covers all the 100 or so commercial series of UK law reports and the newspaper law reports. It also includes practice directions. Updated daily.

3. Badger – A ready-made index, with abstracts, to official publications, including statutes and SIs, press comment and 'grey paper' published since 1994. Updated daily.

4. Legal Journals Index – This is a unique guide to the contents of over 500 UK and English language European legal periodicals – both academic and practitioner titles – covering all aspects of UK and European law and dating back to 1986. Updated daily.

5. Financial Journals Index – This indexes and briefly abstracts the contents of over 85 financial journals in the areas of pensions, banking and insurance and the wider financial services sector, from 1992. Updated daily.

6. Current Law Case Citator – A full judicial history of cases reported since 1977, allowing the progress of a case to be tracked. Updated weekly.

7. Current Law Legislation Citator – A comprehensive guide to amendments to statutes since 89 effected by statute or SI and to changes to SIs since 93. It includes instances of judicial consideration. Updated weekly.

8. Inns of Court Catalogues – A catalogue of catalogues, detailing resources held in the libraries of the Middle and Inner Temples, Gray's Inn and Lincoln's Inn. Updated three times a year. Access to the Inns of Court catalogues is available free of charge. A month's free trial of the service can be arranged.

*New Law Publishing*
http://www.newlawonline.com
New Law Publishing is now a division of Croner Publications. It offers two types of subscription, online and digest. Both cover all areas of law (except Family and Immigration) in the High Court, Court of Appeal, Privy Council, House of Lords, European Court of Justice, Official Referees' Court and Employment Appeal Tribunal.

1. Online facilities – subscribers receive three services in one: (a) daily digests of important English and European Court decisions on the same day as judgment (as above), (b) full text reports of those decisions, and (c) a rapidly growing and easily searchable database. There are more than 4,000 judgments on the system and this number grows daily. The principal benefits are speed, selection using defined criteria, reliability and ease of use.

2. Subscribers receive, by fax or by email, daily case digests only. They do not have the benefit of the database, but full texts are available as and when requested on payment of an additional fee.

*Property Law*
http://www.propertylaw.co.uk
There are two subscription services available: Property Law Service for property
lawyers, and the core EGi service designed for all property professionals.

1. EGi's Property Law Service. This provides property lawyers with essential information about property law immediately (hourly property law news, searchable *Estates Gazette* Law Reports from 1975 to date, Planning Law Reports from 1988 to date, case summaries from a team of barristers from 1988 to date, an *Estates Gazette* archive for

Fig. 14. EGi Property law,
the online service of
*Estates Gazette.*

the last 12 years, *Estates Gazette* Legal Notes from 1984 to date, *Estates Gazette* Planning Notes from 1991 to date, a legislation database, Lands Tribunal database, and writs database. The information is updated daily by a team of journalists and barristers. Around 46 per cent of top UK law firms are said to subscribe.

2.  The core EGi service for all property professionals. This comprises EGi News, an EG archive based on the last 12 years of *Estates Gazette*, Deals (over 19,000 commercial property transactions with up to 250 new deals added a week), Who's Who and Companies Databases containing details of more than 5,500 individuals and 7,000 companies. A library service includes the latest research documents and market reports. A diary service covers what is happening and when. Careers and recruitment advertisements are included for the last four weeks. All property advertisements in the *Estates Gazette* in the last three months are included. EG PropertyLink contains more than 9,000 records searchable by area, type of property, size of property and agency details.

*Web Journal of Current Legal Issues*
http://www.ncl.ac.uk/~nlawwww/
The Web Journal of Current Legal Issues is the first UK web law journal. It focuses on current legal issues in judicial decisions, law reform, legislation, legal research, policy related sociolegal research, legal information, information technology and practice.

In the next chapter we present law associations and the British legal profession on the internet.

# 4 The UK legal profession

**In this chapter we will explore:**

▶ *barristers and advocates*
▶ *solicitors*
▶ *law associations*

This chapter examines the British legal profession and its associations. Since the UK legal profession is divided into two – solicitors and barristers (advocates for the latter in Scotland) – this chapter is divided in the same manner.

## Barristers and advocates

Today there are some 14,000 barristers in England, and around 6,000 advocates in Scotland. Barristers practise in chambers and are governed by the Bar Council.

*The Bar Council*
http://www.barcouncil.org.uk
Based in Bedford Row, London, the Bar Council is the governing body of English barristers. Its web site sets out the origins, history and role of the Bar and includes current contact information, press releases and information about its various activities. The Council deals with the qualification and conduct rules governing barristers and those wishing to become barristers. It deals with complaints against barristers. They say: 'It also puts the Bar's view on matters of concern about the legal system

Fig. 15. The Bar Council web site.

and acts as a source of information about the Bar. This site contains information for a diverse audience: if you are a barrister; a solicitor looking to
instruct a barrister; looking to qualify as a barrister; or a member of the
public, there is information here for you.'

*Bar Directory*
http://www.ftlawandtax.com/bar/index.html
The Bar Directory is published by the General Council of the Bar and FT
Law & Tax. This is the only official directory of UK chambers. It is possible
to search the directory by reference to geographical location, area of specialism, name or language.

*Bar Pro Bono Unit*
http://www.barprobono.org.uk
The Unit was established in May 1996 to provide pro bono – free – legal
advice and representation in deserving cases where legal aid is not available or where the applicant cannot afford legal assistance. Since it
began, over 2,850 applications for assistance have been received, with
help given in more than 1,100 cases. The Unit helps by putting solicitors,
advice agencies and members of the public in touch with barristers
who can give advice – either in writing or in conference – and who can
represent applicants in any court/tribunal in England or Wales

*Butterworth's Legal Directory*
http://www.butterworths.co.uk/bld
Similarly, the Butterworth's Legal Directory is an online version of the
print publication. This is a directory of solicitors and barristers in private
practice, commerce, local government and public authorities in England,
Northern Ireland, Scotland and Wales. You can search the database by
organisation or individual.

*Commercial Bar*
http://www.combar.com
The Commercial Bar web site presents a listing of chambers concerned
mainly or exclusively in serving the commercial market.

*Honourable Society of the Inner Temple*
http://www.innertemple.org.uk
The Honourable Society of the Inner temple, one of the four Inns of
Court, has developed its own web site, covering its membership, scho-
larships, student activities and history.

*Inns of Court*
http://www.online-law.co.uk/bar/inns_of_court.html
The Inns of Court are described here with some interesting history about
each and links to some of the chambers in each.

*Kennedy Guide to Barristers & Expert Witnesses*
http://www.kennedyguidebarristers.com
This is a directory of barristers in the United Kingdom. The site says: 'This

is the first internet directory of its kind that allows barristers to update their entries themselves, as and when changes occur. It also includes attributed endorsements from solicitors. These features help ensure that the user of the guide has the most current information in order to make a more informed choice of counsel.'

*Northern Circuit Commercial Bar Association*
http://www.nccba.org.uk
The Northern Circuit Commercial Bar Association was formed in 1996 to ensure that the skills of the barristers specialising in commercial law who centre their work on the North West of England should be fully recognised within the commercial and business community which they serve.

*Irish Bar Council*
http://www.lawlibrary.ie/barcouncil
The Irish Bar Council is represented on this site.

## Solicitors

Presently, there are more than 70,000 solicitors in the UK. Established as a profession in 1605, solicitors make up the largest of the two branches of the UK legal profession. They have been governed by the Law Society since 1843, and are now governed under the 1974 Solicitors Act.

*Law Society*
http://www.lawsociety.org.uk

Fig. 16. The Law Society online.

Whether you are a solicitor, a citizen, in business, a law student, a trainee, working in a law practice, or just browsing, you will find lots of useful

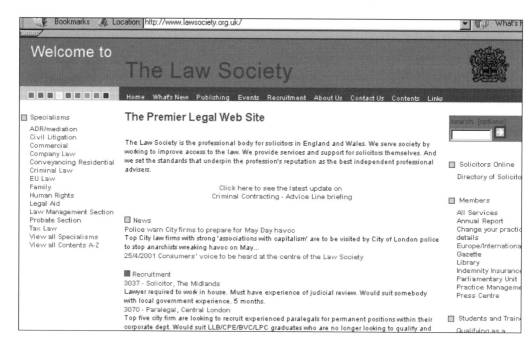

legal information here. The Law Society, the regulatory body for Solicitors in England and Wales, provides information on solicitors, career opportunities, policy notes, and law links. Also you will find the latest edition of the *Law Society Gazette* online and you can search its recruitment ads. There are links to: who we are, legal education, recruitment, directory of solicitors, professional training and accreditation, members services, law and policy, the *Law Society Gazette*, and the office for the supervision of solicitors.

*Law Society of Ireland*
http://www.lawsociety.ie/
The Law Society is the educational, representative and regulatory body of the solicitors' profession in Ireland. It was established in 1773 and now exercises statutory functions under the Solicitors Acts 1954-1994 in relation to the education, admission, enrolment, discipline and regulation of the profession. It works to improve access to the law generally and also provides representation, services and support for solicitors themselves. The Society also deals with complaints from the public about members of the profession and administers a statutory compensation fund. There are currently over 5,000 solicitors practising in Ireland. The web site provides an overview of the work of the solicitors' profession and of The Law Society in Ireland. There are links to education with details on becoming an apprentice and qualifying as a solicitor in Ireland; the *Gazette*, the journal of the Law Society; and links to useful internet sites of interest to legal practitioners.

*Law Society of Scotland*
http://www.lawscot.org.uk
The Law Society of Scotland is the governing body of the solicitor branch of the Scottish legal profession. All practising solicitors in Scotland must be members and take out a practising certificate. All solicitors in private practice and their staff are covered by the Master Policy for Professional Indemnity Insurance which provides protection for the public in respect of loss arising from a solicitor's negligence, failure to observe an undertaking or loss of documents. All principal solicitors in private practice contribute to the Scottish Solicitors Guarantee Fund. The Society has a Council of 50 members, 42 elected by constituents of areas they represent and 8 co-opted from industry, commerce, and central and local government. Council elects annually a President and Vice President. The Society has committees monitoring and developing services in legal education, law reform, professional practice and ethics, complaints handling, professional remuneration, professional indemnity, legal aid, property marketing, international relations, and marketing and public relations.

*Solicitors Online*
http://www.solicitors-online.com
This is a searchable listing of solicitors and firms regulated by the Law Society records. It includes all solicitors who work in private practice law firms and who also have a current practising certificate issued by

the Law Society of England and Wales. You can search by name or by specialism – ADR/mediation, civil litigation, commercial and company law, conveyancing, criminal law, EU law, family law, human rights law, and legal aid. The site includes information on qualifying as a solicitor.

*Solicitors Worldwide*
http://www.pavilion.co.uk/legal/firmgrou.htm
This site provides information on firms of solicitors worldwide, including UK law firms.

## Law associations

*Alliance for Interactive Media Law*
http://www.alliancelaw.com
This is an alliance of United States and European law firms which provide state of the art legal services to the interactive and multimedia industry

*Association of Child Abuse Lawyers*
http://www.abny.demon.co.uk/acal/
The Association and its web site offer practical support for lawyers and other professionals working for adults and children who have been abused. The site gives details of training courses, and a newsletter.

*Association of Commercial Lawyers International*
http://www.acl-int.com
The Association of Commercial Lawyers International (ACL Intl) is a network of 38 firms comprising over 800 lawyers. Member firms around the world offer advice and a global service to clients. ACL offers clients the benefits of local representation in a foreign jurisdiction and local knowledge of cross-border transactions.

*Association of Conditional Fee Lawyers*
http://www.acfl.co.uk
The Association of Conditional Fee Lawyers has been founded to represent the interests of those lawyers who act, or will be acting, in the field of 'no win, no fee'. It has initially been founded to represent the interests of solicitors and may extend to represent the interests of barristers, experts and clients as well.

*Association of Independent European Lawyers*
http://www.aiel.com/
Formed in 1991, in anticipation of the European Open Market, the aim of the Association is to provide a network of independent English speaking legal firms, throughout the European Union, which can refer and interact on behalf of commercial clients across the various legal systems.

*Association of Law Teachers*
http://www.smlawpub.co.uk/academic/alt/About.htm
For membership information see the link to subscriptions. The Association publishes the journal *Law Teacher*.

*Association of Lawyers & Legal Advisors*
http://www.lawyers-assoc.com
The Association of Lawyers & Legal Advisors, the Lawyers' Movement, was founded in April 1995 as an organisation of lawyers, legal advisors or legal service providers operating in a specialised area of law. The main purpose of the association is to accredit members in their specialised area of law by way of a grading system. Accreditation is carried out by senior lawyers in each of the specialised areas of law in which the Association accredits. These certificates of accreditation signed off by a barrister have proved invaluable to lawyers, legal advisors, legal service providers seeking to demonstrate to their customers that they have appropriate expertise in their field.

*Association of Lawyers for Children*
http://www.alc.org.uk
The Association evolved from an idea put forward at the first annual conference organised by child care solicitors and was inaugurated at the third National Conference in Manchester in 1992. Membership includes those lawyers involved in work relating to children – solicitors, barristers and legal staff. The Association also offers associate membership to others involved in working with or for children such as psychiatrists, psychologists, social workers, paediatricians and guardians.

*Association of Pension Lawyers*
http://www.apl.org.uk/
The APL is for lawyers specialising in pensions in the UK. It aims to promote awareness of the importance of the role of pensions law and to operate as a forum for discussion and education amongst pension lawyers. Its members are individuals, not organisations. On this web site, you will find details of who is eligible for membership and application forms if you wish to join. You will also find information about various publications, conferences and training programmes, a diary of events, details of members of the Association's committees and local groups and more.

*Association of Personal Injury Lawyers*
http://www.apil.com/
APIL is dedicated to improving the service provided to victims of accident and clinical negligence. More than 4,500 solicitors and barristers work with the Association to fight for law reform to improve access to justice. This site will be of interest to UK PI lawyers.

*British and Irish Legal Education Technology Association*
http://www.bileta.ac.uk
BILETA was formed in 1986 with the primary objective of promoting technology in legal education throughout the United Kingdom and Ireland, and providing advice and discussion on using technology in legal practice. It works in conjunction with the UK Centre for Legal Education.

*British Legal Association*
http://www.britishlegal.org.uk
The BLA is an association of solicitors, trainee solicitors and barristers drawn from all parts of England and Wales. It was originally formed in 1964 as a protest against Law Society leadership at the time. It publishes a journal, *Independent Solicitor*.

*Employment Lawyers Association*
http://www.elaweb.org.uk
Since its inception in 1992 the ELA has become an authoritative voice on employment law. Its members are qualified lawyers, both barristers and solicitors, practising in employment law in the UK, and organisations engaged in the practice of employment law.

*Euro-American Lawyers Group*
http://www.ealg.com
This is an international network of law firms in the US and Europe. It includes around 365 lawyers working in 21 different jurisdictions from Scandinavia to central America.

*Eurojuris International*
http://www.eurojuris.net
Eurojuris International is a grouping of over 700 law firms in 18 countries throughout Europe and Scandinavia, and covering 650 different cities/locations. The group is composed of 18 national Eurojuris Associations, bringing together medium-sized law firms from each particular country.

*Euro-Link for Lawyers*
http://www.eurolink-law.com
As the title to this site suggests, it offers a Euro link for lawyers. It is one of the largest international legal networks and legal associations in the world. It acts as a facilitator of international legal services bringing together the combined strengths of over 50 commercial legal practices and law firms, with more than 425 partners and 65 offices worldwide.

*European Law Firms*
http://www.european-law-firm.com
This is a grouping of EU law firms and non-EU associate members offering legal services throughout the European Union, and across its internal and external frontiers. It brings together some 250 lawyers practising in all areas of business law.

*Forum of Insurance Lawyers*
http://www.foil.org.uk
FOIL exists to provide a forum for the exchange of information between lawyers acting predominantly or exclusively for insurance clients, either practising within firms of solicitors, as barristers or as in-house lawyers for insurers or for self-insurers.

*Freelance Solicitors Group*
http://members.aol.com/pjmiller00/freelance.html
The Freelance Solicitors Group was originally founded in 1993 as the Locum Solicitors Group. It represents the interests of those solicitors in England and Wales who work as solicitor for others on a locum, contract or freelance basis. The Group maintains a locum list, and organises various social events.

*Immigration Law Practitioners Association*
http://www.ilpa.org.uk
ILPA was established in 1984 by a group of leading UK immigration practitioners. It aims to promote and improve the advising and representation of immigrants, to provide information to members on domestic and European immigration, refugee and nationality law, and to secure a non-racist, non-sexist, just and equitable system of immigration, refugee and nationality law. ILPA has around 900 members including lawyers, advice workers, academics and law students.

*Insolvency Practitioners Association*
http://www.ipa.uk.com/
Founded in 1961, the IPA is the only professional body whose membership comprises solely of insolvency practitioners and who, in the main, act as trustees in bankruptcy, nominees and supervisors of voluntary arrangements, liquidators, administrators and administrative receivers of companies.

*Institute of Trade Mark Attorneys*
http://www.itma.org.uk
ITMA is a professional body dedicated to the protection of trade marks. It considers proposed legislation, offers lectures for members, and promotes honourable practice.

*International Law Association*
http://www.ila-hq.org
The ILA site gives information on International resolutions and treaties from the headquarters of this international non-governmental organisation. The Association's history dates back to 1873 and many of its past and present Officers are leaders in the field of international law.

*International Legal Group*
http://www.intlegalgroup.com
This is a worldwide network of independent law firms. It provides a 'search service for individuals and globalising companies to locate high quality law firms that match their specific needs worldwide. An energy company will have a different legal need than a high-tech software company, and an individual with an estate problem in Brazil, Pakistan or elsewhere will need a totally different law firm – so we look for the right match in each case if we don't already have a member with those skills in the country specified.'

*International Network of Independent Lawyers*
http://www.advoc.com
The web site provides access to legal services across frontiers, throughout Europe, Asia and the Middle East.

*Institute of Legal Executives*
http://www.ilex.org.uk
ILEX is the UK professional body representing over 22,000 legal executives and trainee legal executives. It promotes the profession of legal executive to career advisers, school leavers, graduates, mature students and those contemplating a change of career. Its web site has links to qualification route, the ILEX syllabus, questions answered, study options, and options and opportunities. The site also includes lists of colleges and local branches.

Fig. 17. The Institute of Legal Executives (ILEX), the UK professional body representing legal executives and trainees.

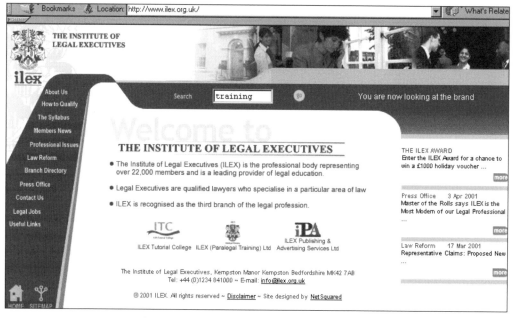

*Jurist: The Legal Education Network*
http://www.law.cam.ac.uk/jurist/index.htm
This is a very useful legal education network hosted by the University of Cambridge Faculty of Law. The web site covers UK law schools, prospectuses, staff, and libraries; law school news with clippings and reports on legal education; resources for UK law teachers; and tips for law students and more.

*Justices' Clerk's Society*
http://www.jc-society.co.uk
The Society was founded in 1839 and incorporated in 1903. It is a professional body representing the principal legal advisers to lay magistrates in England and Wales and is committed to improving the quality of justice in magistrates' courts. One of its main objects is to review the operation of the law, especially that administered by magis-

trates' courts in England and Wales, to point out its defects and to encourage proposals for improvement.

*Law Centres Federation*
http://www.lawcentres.org.uk
The Federation encourages the development of publicly funded legal services for those most disadvantaged in society and promotes the Law Centre model as the best means of achieving this. Centres offer free and independent professional legal advice to local people. The site lists the addresses of local offices and contains links to many organisations concerned with issues such as benefits, equal opportunities, health and housing, disability, and immigration.

*Legal Action Group*
http://www.lag.org.uk
LAG is a national independent charity which campaigns for equal access to justice for all members of society. It provides support to the practice of lawyers and advisers; inspires developments in that practice; campaigns for improvements in the law and the administration of justice; and stimulates debate on how services should be delivered.

*Magistrates Association*
http://www.magistrates-association.org.uk
The Magistrates' Association is a registered UK charity and the body which represents the 30,000 magistrates – Justices of the Peace as they are also known – in England and Wales. This new web site provides general information on how to become a magistrate, about what JPs do, and magistrates in the community. It also features a members' page where magistrates can exchange ideas and provoke discussion. Training and membership issues are also discussed.

*Medico-Legal Society*
http://www.medico-legalsociety.org.uk
Founded in 1901, the Society aims to promote medico-legal knowledge in all its aspects. Its official organ is the *Medico-Legal Journal*.

*Motor Accident Solicitors Society*
http://www.mass.org.uk
MASS is an association of solicitors' firms, all with experience and expertise in the handling of motor accident claims. Member firms are located throughout the UK.

*National Association of Paralegals*
http://ourworld.compuserve.com/homepages/napl/
The Association offers a careers and qualifications route for those who for one reason or another do not qualify as a solicitor or a barrister in the UK. The main qualification is its Associate Qualification (Advanced Award in Paralegal Studies), which is run on an evening course basis by colleges throughout the UK.

*Society for Computers and Law*
http://www.scl.org
The SCL exists to encourage and develop both information technology for lawyers and IT-related law. The web site contains details of its local branches, working groups, publications and more. Its membership now exceeds 2,000 and encompasses everyone from members of he judiciary to lawyers, teachers and IT managers.

*Society of Public Teachers of Law*
http://www.law.warwick.ac.uk/sptl/
The SPTL is the learned society of university lecturers. Founded in 1908, it gathers law academics together (your tutors do have friends, after all!). It aims to advance legal education, which includes teaching in universities, legal research and the professional training of lawyers. It organises a programme of seminars and has about twenty subject sections for members with particular legal interests.

*Society of Trust and Estate Practitioners*
http://www.step.org
The site of the Society of Trust and Estate Practitioners provides discussion pages and guidance on the latest property law.

*Sole Practitioners Group*
http://www.spg.uk.com
This is web site about solicitors who practise on their own account without partners. They may or may not employ other solicitor staff. Most of them have their own firms serving clients on a personal basis. There are about 4,800 sole practitioner solicitors in England and Wales.

*Solicitors Family Law Association*
http://www.sfla.org.uk
SFLA is an association of over 5,000 solicitors, started in 1982, whose members believe that aggressive lawyers and reliance on the court process can add to distress and anger on the breakdown of a family relationship. SFLA members abide by a code of practice designed to promote a conciliatory atmosphere in which matters are dealt with in a sensitive, constructive and cost-effective way.

*UK Environmental Law Association*
http://www.greenchannel.com/ukela/
The Association is not only open to lawyers. Many of its 1,000 or so members are scientists and others involved with environmental law, both in the UK and overseas.

In Part Two of this handbook, we provide reviews of web sites on legal practice areas.

# 5 European, human rights and international law

**In this chapter we will explore:**

▶ *European law online*
▶ *human rights and immigration law online*
▶ *international law online*

## European law online

*Danish Bar and Law Society*
http://www.advocom.dk/advsamuk.html
Information on the Danish Bar and Law Society are given on this site.

*European Court of Justice*
http://europa.eu.int/index-en.htm
As noted above in Chapters 2 and 3, the ECJ can be accessed using this site and its case law traced and downloaded. See also:

http://europa.eu.int/cj/en/index.htm

*European Court of Human Rights*
http://www.echr.coe.int
This page marks the home of the European Court of Human Rights in Strasbourg. The ECHR is the guardian and interpreter of the 1950 European Convention on Human Rights. This site gives you access to case law, legislation, opinions, a short history of the Court, and an explanation of its function.

Fig. 18. The web site of the European Court of Human Rights.

49

# European, human rights and international law ........................

*European Information Association*
http://www.hull.ac.uk/php/lbsebd/eia_html/access1.htm
The University of Hull acts as the link-way to the European Information Association's site, giving up-to-date news from the EU institutions on all matters of policy.

*European Law Office*
http://www.europeanlawoffice.com
The European Law Office is a very useful site, providing access to legal news as it emerges, as well as commentaries on current EU law.

*Goodbody*
http://www.algoodbody.ie/dbi/legal
This Irish law firm's web site provides excellent commentaries on the Irish legal system. In particular, it provides information on business law, property law, environment and labour/employment law.

*ICCL: The European Legal 500*
http://www.icclaw.com/lfe/europe.htm
This is a well-organised collection of links to some 3,000 recommended law firms and lawyers (excluding England and Wales) developed and maintained by the International Centre for Commercial Law. The section for each country includes an overview (billing system, general notes, the economic climate and the legal market), links to recommended firms, a law firm directory, major firms by size, legal developments, and proprietary web sites.

*Irish Law*
http://www.ucc.ie/ucc/depts/law/irishlaw
This site, hosted by Ireland's University College Cork, provides wide-ranging sources and discussion on Irish law, including Irish Constitutional and European law. It also gives miscellaneous Irish legal links to Irish legal institutions, Irish law associations, libraries, case law and legal academics and practitioners. Its Irish law archives are very useful research tools for UK practitioners looking up points of Irish law, as are its Irish law FAQs file.

*Institute for European Law*
http://www.iel.bham.ac.uk/
The Institute for European Law, hosted by the University of Birmingham provides many useful links to other European law sites.

*Law Firms in Europe*
http://www.european-law-firm.com/links.htm
This hyperlink site gives access to law firms in Europe which specialise in European law. Some of these firms have updating services on their sites and offer case law commentaries.

## Human rights and immigration law online

*1 Crown Office Row Chambers*
http://www.onecrownofficerow.com/hru/index.htm
This chambers' site from 1 Crown Office Row includes specialist barristers in immigration law. It gives a Human Rights Act 1998 update. It also discusses and offers services on the Human Rights Act, Human Rights Convention and Strasbourg law – legal documents of fundamental importance to lawyers preparing cases when the Act comes into force.

*Citizens Advice Bureaux*
http://www.nacab.org.uk
Local Citizens Advice Bureaux (CABs) and their national sister organisation, the National Association of Citizens Advice Bureaux (NACAB), offer a wide-range of information and statistical research on today's salient social issues, for example poverty, exclusion, money advice, debts, housing and social security benefits.

*Electronic Immigration Network*
http://www.ein.org.uk
The EIN is a charity relating to immigration, refugee and nationality law and practice in the UK. Its site contains a comprehensive list of links to other sites related to immigration and human rights issues, both in this country and around the world (take 'Resources'). A subscription service offers access to all Immigration Appeal Tribunal determinations and relevant reports from higher courts. The service is designed to assist all practitioners working in the field of immigration, refugee and asylum law; researchers, advocates, representatives, welfare advice workers, teachers and the adjudicators themselves. The objectives of the project are:

1.  The speedy provision of accurate and up-to-date information.

Fig. 19. The Electronic Immigration Network.

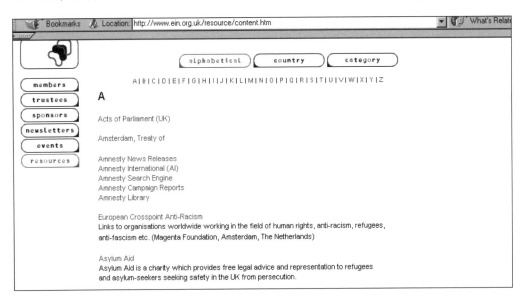

2. The creation of a members' community of shared interests, enabling communication and cross fertilisation of ideas and best practice.

Free services include a set of links to immigration-related sites world wide, plus events listings with details of conferences, seminars and new publications. Relevant organisations can advertise their events free. Subscription services include the full text of immigration tribunal determinations, continuously updated with the most recent cases and indexed with more than 800 keywords. The database can also be searched by text, date, court, judge, location and by decision. It now contains more than 3,000 Immigration Tribunal determinations and other case reports and summaries from the higher Courts. The Tribunal determinations represent the core material of current jurisprudence on immigration and asylum law. EIN bulletin boards include:

eincaselaw – for the latest determinations
einnews – for news and events
einqueries – for members' questions and answers
eintech – for technical queries.

*Electronic Frontier Foundation*
http://www.eff.com

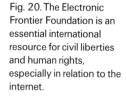

Fig. 20. The Electronic Frontier Foundation is an essential international resource for civil liberties and human rights, especially in relation to the internet.

The Electronic Frontier Foundation is a substantial international archive of human rights and civil liberties issues, and is sponsor of the Blue Ribbon campaign for freedom of speech on the internet. It gives up-to-date information on borders control and migration policies. This is particularly good for 'Schengen' watchers.

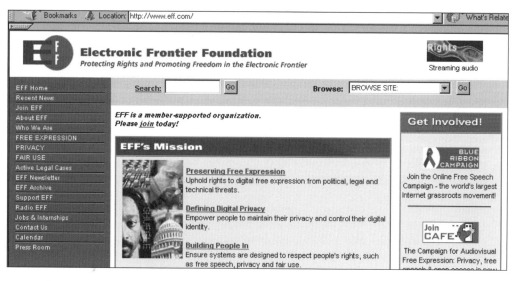

*Human Rights Web*
http://www.hrweb.org
The Human Rights Web offers a comprehensive service of advice, information and references on immigration and human rights law.

*Immigration Advisory Service*

http://www.vois.org.uk/ias/

The Immigration Advisory Service describes itself as the largest and most experienced charity giving free advice and representation in immigration and asylum matters. It has regional offices in Birmingham, Cardiff, Central London, Gatwick, Glasgow, Hounslow, Leeds and Manchester. The IAS deals with over 7,500 appeals and 20,000 telephone enquiries every year. An IAS duty counsellor is available 24 hours a day.

*Immigration Law Practitioners' Association*

http://www.ein.org.uk/ilpa/

The Immigration Law Practitioners' Association (better known as ILPA) is the UK's professional association of lawyers and academics practising in or concerned about immigration, asylum and nationality law. Its membership currently stands at 650. Membership is by application supported by two references and subject to an annual membership fee. It is only open to persons subject to a professional disciplinary body. Immigration Law relating to English speaking countries is provided by BCL Immigration Services. There is also a collection of privacy and encryption material.

*Law Links*

http://www.ukc.ac.uk/library/lawlinks/

Law Links is an excellent annotated list of web sites compiled by Sarah Carter at the University of Kent at Canterbury. Follow the link to European Union for some excellent and well-organised official and unofficial resources for European Union law and current affairs.

Fig. 21. Law Links guide to International Law.

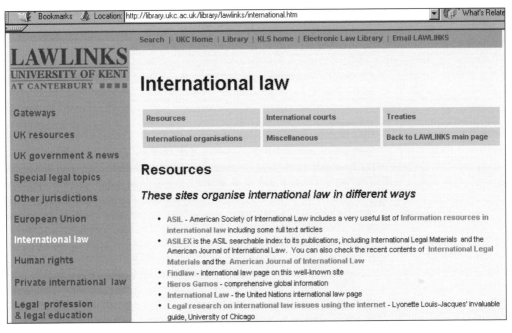

*Legal Action Group*
http://www.lag.org.uk
LAG is the national independent charity which campaigns for equal access to justice for all members of society, provides support to lawyers and advisers, inspires developments in that practice, and campaigns for improvements in the law.

*RightsNet*
http://www.rightsnet.org.uk/discuss/
The RightsNet site provides support and information about welfare rights to advice workers, including legislative changes, policy and case law developments. It is maintained by the London Advice Services Alliance.

## International law online

*American Society of International Law*
http://www.asil.org
This Washington-based organisation offers a publications database and numerous links.

*Australasian Legal Information Institute*
http://www.austlii.edu.au
The site provides free internet access to Australian legal materials. It has grown into one of the largest sources of legal materials on the net, with over seven gigabytes of raw text materials and over 1.5 million searchable documents.

*Canadian Bar Association*
http://www.algonquinc.on.ca/cba/
This is the dual-language web site of the Canadian Bar Association (l'Association du Barreau Canadien).

*Canadian Department of Justice*
http://canada.justice.gc.ca/en/index.html

*CataLaw*
http://www.catalaw.com
CataLaw is an ambitious catalogue of catalogues of worldwide law on the Internet. It aids legal research by arranging all indexes of law and government into a uniform, universal and unique metaindex. You can explore the material by region, by topic (from aviation and space law to women and gender law) and certain other criteria. There are also international links to continuing legal education, expert directories, general legal education, internet discussion lists, law libraries and publishers, law practice management, law school lists, law societies and associations, legal directories, legal employment, legal periodicals and legal research.

*Cornell Legal Information Institute*
http://www.law.cornell.edu/
This is an excellent collection of mainly American material, along with some worldwide links.

*Interleges*
http://www.interleges.com
Interleges is an international association of independent law firms, with offices across the countries of the European Union, eastern Europe, North America, the middle east and in other key commercial regions of the world. Its web site offers addresses and contact points.

*International Bar Association*
http://www.ibanet.org
The International Bar Association was founded in 1947 and is the world's largest international organisation of Law Societies, Bar Associations and individual lawyers engaged in international law. It is composed of over 18,000 individual lawyer members in 183 countries and 173 Law Societies and Bar Associations together representing more than 2.5 million lawyers.

*International Centre for Commercial Law*
http://www.icclaw.com
The ICCL provides information on lawyers and law firms throughout the UK, Europe and Asia and the Pacific. The UK section includes access to an electronic version of the Legal 500 and provides information on a wide range of UK law firms.

*International Association of Constitutional Law*
http://www.eur.nl/iacl/index.html
The IACL allows for trans-national and global discussion of contemporary constitutional issues.

*International Court of Justice*
http://www.icj-cij.org
The ICJ is the principal judicial organ of the United Nations, based at the Peace Palace in
The Hague (Netherlands). It began work in 1946, replacing the Permanent Court of International Justice. The Court has a dual role: to settle in accordance with international law the legal disputes submitted to it by States, and to give advisory opinions on legal questions referred to it by authorised international organs and agencies. The web site includes the full texts of cases from 1996 onwards.

*International Criminal Court*
http://www.un.org/law/icc
In July 1998 the international community met in Rome to finalise a draft statute which, when ratified, will establish such a court to prosecute crimes of utmost gravity such as genocide

*International Law Association*
http://www.ila-hq.org/
The ILA was founded in Brussels in 1873. Its objectives include the study and advancement of international law, public and private, the study of comparative law, the making of proposals for the solution of conflicts of

law and for the unification of law, and the furthering of international understanding and goodwill. Its 3,700-strong membership ranges from lawyers in private practice, academia, government and the judiciary, to non-lawyer experts from commercial, industrial and financial spheres.

*International Law Commission*
http://www.un.org/law/ilc/index.htm
The ILC was established by the General Assembly in 1947 to promote the progressive development of international law and its codification. The Commission, which meets annually, is composed of 34 members who are elected by the General Assembly for five year terms and who serve in their individual capacity, not as representatives of their governments. There are links to Commission Reports and other documentation.

*International Network of Independent Lawyers*
http://www.advoc.com
INIL is an organisation providing access to legal services across frontiers, throughout Europe, Asia and the Middle East.

*Kimes International Law Directory*
http://www.ftlawandtax.com/kimes/index.html
The Kimes International Law Directory is a worldwide directory of lawyers containing up-to-date information on approximately 650 law firms and chambers in around 250 countries.

*Law.com*
http://www.law.com
Based in San Francisco, Law.com provides a current legal news service, seminars, services, and more. It claims to be the web's most comprehensive legal destination and provider of legal application solutions. Through its multiple offerings, it aims to help you manage your practice with web-based and desktop applications, track breaking developments in the law, research issues and cases, attend online continuing legal education seminars, explore US-wide job openings in the legal industry, and more. They say: 'We provide the legal community with the tools and intelligence to compete and succeed in today's wired world.'

*Law Links*
http://www.ukc.ac.uk/library/lawlinks/
Law Links is an excellent annotated list of web sites compiled by Sarah Carter at the University of Kent at Canterbury. Follow the link to International Law for treaties, international courts and international organisations. Follow the link to Private International Law for international commercial law, international trade, maritime law and other resources.

*Legal 500*
The section for each country includes an overview (billing system, general notes, the economic climate and the legal market), links to recommended firms, a law firm directory, major firms by size, legal devel-

opments, and proprietary web sites. The material is developed and maintained by the International Centre for Commercial Law:

| | |
|---|---|
| Asia Pacific | http://www.icclaw.com/as500/asia.htm |
| Middle East | http://www.icclaw.com/lfe/middle-e.htm |
| USA | http://www.icclaw.com/us500/usa.htm |

*Lexadin*
http://www.lexadin.nl
The Lexadin World Law Guide contains more than 4,000 links to legal sites in more than 40 countries, though the material does not appear to have been updated recently.

*Logos*
http://www.logos-eeig.com
Logos is a network of independent law firms in Europe. With one law firm in each of twelve countries of the European Union and contacts in the other three, Logos aims to assist any business or law firm around the world that needs legal support in Europe.

# 6 Criminal justice & civil litigation

**In this chapter we will explore:**

▶ *criminal law texts and links*
▶ *criminal law institutions online*
▶ *civil justice reforms*
▶ *consumer law resources online*

The rate of crime continues to increase. Criminal law covers the offences against the State for wrongdoing. Civil law covers the actions and remedies available under the law of tort and contract. Consequently, this chapter seeks only to cover more general issues of concern to civil law practitioners, such as the 'Woolf Reforms' and the latest developments in civil law.

## Criminal law texts and links

*British Journal of Criminology*
http://www.oup.co.uk/crimin/
Published by Oxford University Press (OUP), the British Journal of Criminology web site provides articles and news on current developments in criminal law.

*Criminal Law Links*
http://snipe.ukc.ac.uk/law/spu/crimjust.htm
This criminal law links site has been developed at the University of Kent. It gives criminal practitioners access to statutes, case law, journals and other commentaries on criminal law.

*Criminal Law Review*
http://elj.warwick.ac.uk/juk/journals/clr1.html
The site, hosted by the University of Warwick, gives information and access to the *Criminal Law Review* the leading journal for criminal law academics. Its frequency is monthly.

*Howard League for Penal Reform*
http://web.ukonline.co.uk/howard.league/
The Howard League was established in 1866, and named after John Howard, the founder of the penal reform movement. An independent charity, it works for humane, effective, and efficient reform of the penal system. The site contains information about events, news, publications and links.

*NACRO*
http://www.nacro.org.uk
This is the web site of the National Association for the Care and Rehabilitation of Offenders.

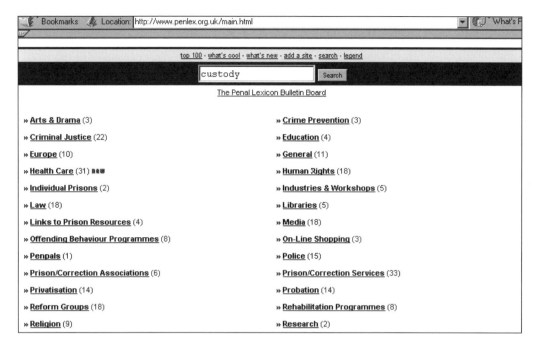

The Penal Lexicon Bulletin Board

| | |
|---|---|
| » **Arts & Drama** (3) | » **Crime Prevention** (3) |
| » **Criminal Justice** (22) | » **Education** (4) |
| » **Europe** (10) | » **General** (11) |
| » **Health Care** (31) **new** | » **Human Rights** (18) |
| » **Individual Prisons** (2) | » **Industries & Workshops** (5) |
| » **Law** (18) | » **Libraries** (5) |
| » **Links to Prison Resources** (4) | » **Media** (18) |
| » **Offending Behaviour Programmes** (8) | » **On-Line Shopping** (3) |
| » **Penpals** (1) | » **Police** (15) |
| » **Prison/Correction Associations** (6) | » **Prison/Correction Services** (33) |
| » **Privatisation** (14) | » **Probation** (14) |
| » **Reform Groups** (18) | » **Rehabilitation Programmes** (8) |
| » **Religion** (9) | » **Research** (2) |

*Penal Lexicon*
http://www.penlex.org.uk
According to the Penal Lexicon, to pretend that society's ills will be solved if we just 'lock 'em up and throw away the key' is to ignore the experience, the research and the expertise that already exists in the British penal system. This UK-based site holds an enormous amount of information on prison service structure, policies, rules, parole matters, statistics, annual reports, services for prisoners' families and miscarriages of justice. It is unafraid to have an opinion and pleads for a complex analysis of these problems.

*Police Law*
http://www.policelaw.co.uk
The site is a substantial portal to police and law related sites, pointing readers in the direction of new laws, law books and case decisions. There are main links to policing law, law updates, official information, police links, and police forces of the UK.

*Prisons Handbook*
http://www.tphbook.demon.co.uk
This site offers an online Prisons Handbook, a definitive annual guide to the penal system of England and Wales. It has become established as the principal source of reference for the penal system of England and Wales since the first edition appeared in 1995. In 1996 the Prison Service instructed the governors of all prisons and young offender institutions in England and Wales to stock it in both their inmate and staff libraries. It is also a required text on many law and criminology courses.

Fig. 22. Penlex.

*Youth Justice and Criminal Evidence Act 1999*
http://www.hmso.gov.uk/acts/en/1999en23.htm
The site contains the text of the Youth Justice and Criminal Evidence Act 1999. This is accompanied by explanatory notes prepared by the Home Office to assist the reader in understanding the Act.

▶ *Note* – Archbold, *Criminal Pleading, Evidence and Practice*, and Blackstone's *Criminal Law,* are both available now on CD, but you will still have to continue, for the moment at least, taking either your laptop or voluminous paper copies to court, as neither are on the net yet!

## Criminal law institutions

*Court Service*
http://www.courtservice.gov.uk/cs-home.htm
As noted above, the Court Service is an executive agency of the Lord Chancellor's Department. It provides administrative support to the courts and tribunals within the UK. It offers criminal law practitioners with a list of courts and accessible cases transcripts.

*Criminal Cases Review Commission*
http://www.ccrc.gov.uk
The Criminal Cases Review Commission independently investigates any alleged miscarriages of Justice. Its site provides guidance and forms on how to complain.

*Criminal Courts Review*
http://www.criminal-courts-review.org.uk/
This is the official site for Lord Justice Auld's review of working of the criminal justice system. The site includes press notices and the latest progress reports.

*Criminal Injuries Compensation Authority*
http://www.cica.gov.uk
In 1996 the CICA was established to administer the tariff-based scheme which came into effect for all applications received on or after 1 April 1996. The web site is designed to provide information about the scheme and to help potential applicants apply for compensation and complete a personal injury or fatal injury application form.

*Crown Prosecution Service*
http://www.cps.gov.uk/home_page.htm
Created by the Prosecution of Offences Act 1985, the CPS is the government department which prosecutes people in England and Wales who have been charged by the police with a criminal offence. Within each of its 42 local areas are one or more branch offices handling local prosecutions and headed by a Branch Crown Prosecutor. In 1997-98, the branches dealt with 1.4 million cases in the Magistrates' Courts and 128,064 in the Crown Courts. The site provides information on senten-

cing, CPS Codes, its various offices, case updates, a news desk, an annual report and other publications. The site includes a Welsh language version.

*European Court of Human Rights*
http://www.dhcour.coe.int
The European Court of Human Rights site, as noted above, gives information on enforcing and interpreting the rights of citizens held under the 1950 European Convention on Human Rights. This will become more important to criminal practitioners after 2 November 2000 with the enactment and coming into force of the 1998 Human Rights Act. This site will be of immense value.

*Forensic Science Service*
http://www.forensic.gov.uk
The Forensic Science Service supplies forensic science services to police forces in England and Wales, and is a source of training, consultancy, and scientific support for many overseas and private sector customers, including law enforcement agencies in 60 countries worldwide.

*Her Majesty's Prison Service*
http://www.open.gov.uk/prison
Her Majesty's Prison Service serves the public by keeping in custody those committed by the courts, organises and administers the British prison system. Its web site apparently attracts around 34,000 hits per month. There is a link to Her Majesty's Chief Inspector of Prisons for England and Wales.

*Home Office*
http://www.homeoffice.gov.uk
The Home Office is the government department responsible for internal affairs in England and Wales. Its main business is law and order. The home page has links to constitutional and community issues, human rights, race equality, freedom of information, data protection, elections, political parties and European issues, crime reduction, the latest crime figures, criminal justice, prisons, the police, probation and courts, the emergency services, disaster management, immigration, and passports. This site provides invaluable information on criminal law to practitioners.

*Law Commission*
http://www.gtnet.gov.uk/lawcomm/
The Law Commission is the statutory law reform body in the UK. Its site gives information on the latest Law Reform proposals. It contains some useful information on 'corporate manslaughter'.

*Lord Chancellor's Department: Criminal Matters*
http://www.open.gov.uk/lcd/criminal/crimfr.htm
This site gives details of guidance, policy initiatives and recent case law and statutes affecting criminal law. This site provides the latest information from the Lord Chief Justice.

# Criminal justice & civil litigation .......................................

Bookmarks  Location: http://www.open.gov.uk/lcd/criminal/crimfr.htm    What's Rela

THE LORD CHANCELLOR'S DEPARTMENT

## Criminal Matters

● **The Government's Criminal Justice Strategy**

   ● *Criminal Justice - The Way Ahead*: modernising the criminal justice system [26 February 2001]
   ● The Home Secretary's Statement in the House of Commons [26 February 2001]
   ● Press Notice: *Fit for the Future - Modernising the Criminal Justice System* [26 February 2001]

● **The Trials Issues Group (TIG)**

   ● What is the Trials Issues Group? [September 2000]
   ● Criminal Justice Consultative Council & the Trials Issue Group [September 2000]
   ● *TIG Update* - the Trials Issue Group Newsletter

● Evaluation of the Youth Court Demonstration Project + press notice
   [13 December 2000]

● Guide to the Criminal Justice System in England and Wales [23 October 2000]

Fig. 23. The Lord Chancellor's web site: Criminal Matters.

*Metropolitan Police*
http://www.open.gov.uk/police/metpol/methome.htm
This is the official site of the London Metropolitan Police. As part of the CCTA Government Information Service, this must surely be just the beginning of getting the police online. There is some useful information on the River Police and tips for using marine craft on the Thames. Otherwise, at the moment, there is nothing about Operation Eagle Eye or a hotlink to the Police Complaints Authority.

*National Criminal Intelligence Service*
http://www.ncis.co.uk/
NCIS works to combat serious crime, in conjunction with law enforcement agencies, government departments and other relevant organisations both nationally and internationally.

*National Probation Directorate*
http://www.homeoffice.gov.uk/cpg/probu2.htm
The Directorate exercises on behalf of the Home Secretary all his responsibilities for the probation service in England and Wales. It serves the courts and the public by supervising offenders in the community, helping offenders to lead law-abiding lives, and safeguarding the welfare of children in family proceedings. The probation service operates locally under area probation committees or boards within a framework of national standard.

*Police Complaints Authority*
http://www.pca.gov.uk
The PCA is an independent body set up by the Government to oversee

public complaints against police officers in the 43 police services in England and Wales, plus the British Transport, Ministry of Defence, and certain other forces. It can investigate complaints made by members of the public or referred directly by police services.

*Youth Justice Board for England and Wales*
http://www.youth-justice-board.gov.uk
The Youth Justice Board for England and Wales, is a new executive non-departmental public body established on 30 September 1998 under the Crime and Disorder Act 1998, to advise on the supervision and administration of youth justice within England and Wales.

## Civil justice reforms

*Civil Justice Reform: Implementation*
http://www.open.gov.uk/lcd/civil/progrfr.htm
This site considers the implementation of the Civil Justice Reform and gives some progress reports.

Fig. 24. The Lord Chancellor's web site: the Woolf Reforms.

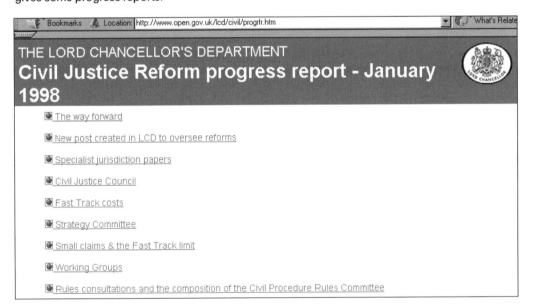

Justice Reform: Report
http://www.open.gov.uk/lcd/civil/inter.htm
This site presents the UK Government Information Service's Report on Civil Justice Reform.

*Woolf Report and Commentary*
http://www.open.gov.uk/lcd/civil/interim/chap23.htm
The Woolf Report is reproduced on this site, along with expert commentary.

*Woolf Reforms: Civil Litigation*
http://www.open.gov.uk/lcd/civil/interim/woolf.htm
Here you can find out about the Woolf Report, more commonly known

as *Access to Justice*, authored by Lord Woolf in July 1996. This sets out the detailed Woolf Reforms which affect civil litigation

▶ *Note* – The Court Rules, like their predecessors the Green and White Books – are still only available on CD and are not yet available on the internet.

## Consumer law

*Consumer Gateway*
http://www.consumer.gov.uk
The Consumer Gateway provides advice, Government reports, and information on cars, finance, food, home improvement and utilities. It also explains how to complain and to which bodies.

*Office of Fair Trading*
http://www.oft.gov.uk
The OFT site provides not only commentaries on relevant law and legal developments, but also information on how to take action under civil law. It contains links to various consumer advice groups. You will also find its annual report, news stories, press releases and articles from *Fair Trading* magazine.

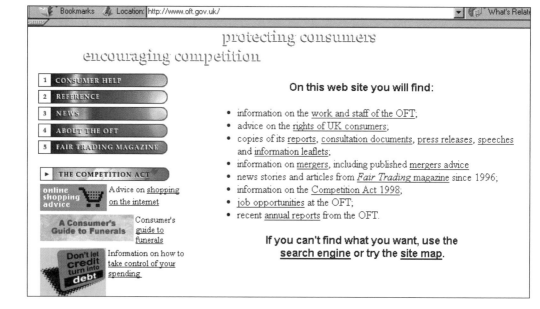

*Trading Standards*
http://www.tradingstandards.gov.uk
This is an official one-stop shop for consumer protection information in the UK. It provides a wealth of information for consumers and businesses, schools, advice and information centres, community organisations, busi-

ness support agencies and trade associations. You can use the site to contact your local trading standards service for advice and information. Just type your postcode in the box provided and press Find, and you should see a hyperlink to your local office.

▶ See also – *Shops and Shopping on the Internet* by Kathy Lambert. A practical guide to online stores, catalogues, retailers and shopping malls. A free illustrated catalogue is available from the publishers (see back cover for details).

# 7 Employment, family & social welfare law

**In this chapter we will explore:**

▶ *employment laws and regulations*
▶ *employment law institutions*
▶ *employment law research sites*
▶ *family law sources*
▶ *mediation*
▶ *social security law*
▶ *pressure groups and networks*

In this chapter we review three growing legal areas of social importance – employment, family and social welfare law. For immigration law see chapter 5, European, human rights and international law.

## Employment laws and regulations

*The Stationery Office: Acts*
http://www.hmso.gov.uk/acts.htm
The Stationery Office, formerly the HMSO, the Queen's Official Publishers, publishes on its site the full text of Acts as enacted from January 1996. This site makes a very useful starting point for tracing the latest version of Acts. It also includes Bills before parliament, another useful means of monitoring future legal changes.

Fig. 26. The Stationery Office has Acts of Parliament online.

Bookmarks    Netsite: http://www.hmso.gov.uk/acts/acts2000.htm    Wha

## Public Acts

- Northern Ireland Act 2000 c.1
- Representation of the People Act 2000 c.2
- Consolidated Fund Act 2000 c.3
- Armed Forces Discipline Act 2000 c.4
- Nuclear Safeguards Act 2000 c.5
- Powers of Criminal Courts (Sentencing) Act 2000 c.6
- Electronic Communications Act 2000 c.7
- Financial Services and Markets Act 2000 c.8
- Appropriation Act 2000 c.9
- Crown Prosecution Inspectorate Act 2000 c.10
- The Terrorism Act 2000 c.11
- Limited Liability Partnerships Act 2000 c.12
- Royal Parks (Trading) Act 2000 c.13
- Care Standards Act 2000 c.14

*The Stationery Office: Statutory Instruments*
http://www.hmso.gov.uk/stat.htm
As with the above-mentioned site for Acts, this site conveniently only covers the increasing number of Statutory Instruments, providing their full texts from 1997.

*New Law Publishing*
http://www.newlawonline.com
New Law Publishing is now a division of Croner Publications, the employment law specialists. It offers two types of subscriptions: Online and Digest, covering all areas of law (except Family and Immigration) in the High Court, Court of Appeal, Privy Council, House of Lords, European Court of Justice, Official Referees' Court and Employment Appeal Tribunal. Online subscribers receive three services in one:

1. Daily digests of important English and European Court decisions on the same day as judgment (as above).

2. Full text reports of those decisions.

3. A rapidly growing and easily searchable database. There are more than 4,000 judgments on the system and this number grows daily. It offers the benefits of speed, selection using defined criteria, reliability, and ease of use.

Subscribers receive daily case digests only by fax or email. They do not have the benefit of the database, but full texts are available as and when requested on payment of an additional fee.

*Tolley*
http://www.tolley.co.uk
Founded in 1916, Tolley Publishing is a leading publisher of tax, legal and business publications in the UK. It provides information in a variety of formats including looseleafs, textbooks, journals, newsletters, magazines and CD-ROMs. These are aimed at legal, tax and accountancy practitioners, directors, managers, administrators, in-house professionals and corporate officers in the commercial and local government sectors.

## Employment law institutions

*Arbitration, Conciliation and Advisory Service*
http://www.acas.org.uk
ACAS offers guidance on dispute resolution and on various employment regulations.

*Chartered Institute of Personnel & Development*
http://www.cipd.co.uk
The Institute of Personnel & Development is the recently chartered institute of HR practitioners. It provides advice and information to personnel professionals, produces codes of good practice, and has pages on professional development information, especially on courses run throughout the year (including its Advanced Certificate on Employment Law), and lists local branch contact details.

*Confederation of British Industry*
http://www.cbi.org.uk
The CBI is a representative body for employers. It gives advice to firms on good practice and commentary on employment laws.

*Commission for Racial Equality*
http://www.open.gov.uk/cre/crehome.htm
The CRE's site explains its role, powers and guidance on how to eliminate racial discrimination.

*Department of Trade and Industry*
http://www.dti.gov.uk
The DTI is the Government department charged with competition and employment regulation. Within the site are pages on:

Employment regulation
Useful contacts
The latest ministerial speeches
Consultation documents on employment matters

*Discrimination Law Association*
http://www.parish.oaktree.co.uk/dla/dla1.htm
This peculiarly titled site is the home page of the Discrimination Law Association, giving commentaries on the latest cases and other data in relation to disability, race, gender, sexuality and age discrimination.

*Employment Appeal Tribunal*
http://www.employmentappeals.gov.uk
The Employment Appeal Tribunal (EAT) has a new web site providing case transcripts, case listings (very useful for the employment law practitioner) and forms for appeals and notices.

Fig. 27. The web site of the Employment Appeal Tribunal.

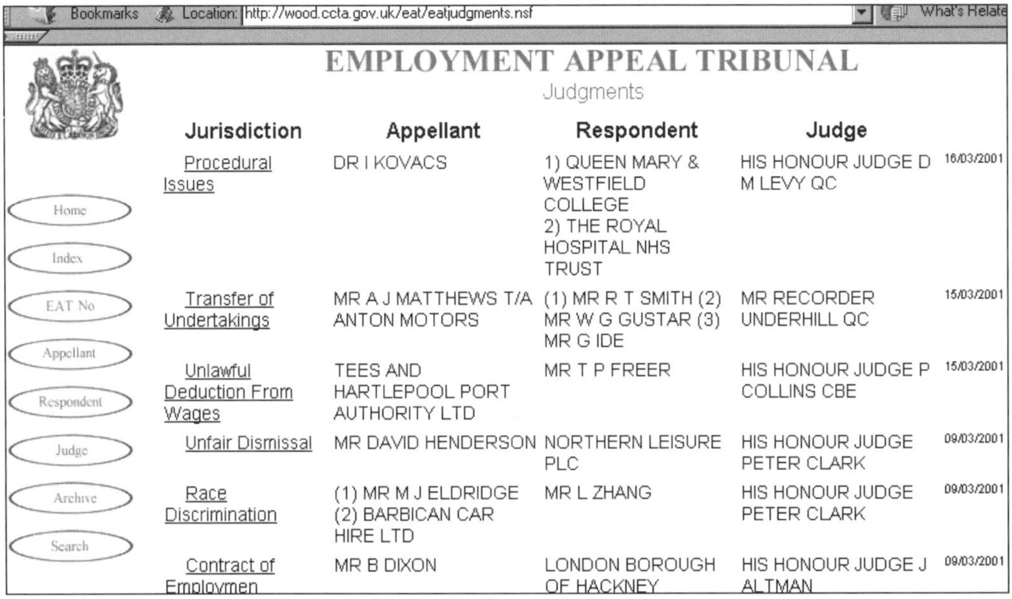

Bookmarks   Location: http://wood.ccta.gov.uk/eat/eatjudgments.nsf   What's Relate

## EMPLOYMENT APPEAL TRIBUNAL
Judgments

| | Jurisdiction | Appellant | Respondent | Judge | |
|---|---|---|---|---|---|
| Home | Procedural Issues | DR I KOVACS | 1) QUEEN MARY & WESTFIELD COLLEGE 2) THE ROYAL HOSPITAL NHS TRUST | HIS HONOUR JUDGE D M LEVY QC | 16/03/2001 |
| Index | | | | | |
| EAT No | Transfer of Undertakings | MR A J MATTHEWS T/A ANTON MOTORS | (1) MR R T SMITH (2) MR W G GUSTAR (3) MR G IDE | MR RECORDER UNDERHILL QC | 15/03/2001 |
| Appellant | | | | | |
| Respondent | Unlawful Deduction From Wages | TEES AND HARTLEPOOL PORT AUTHORITY LTD | MR T P FREER | HIS HONOUR JUDGE P COLLINS CBE | 15/03/2001 |
| Judge | Unfair Dismissal | MR DAVID HENDERSON | NORTHERN LEISURE PLC | HIS HONOUR JUDGE PETER CLARK | 09/03/2001 |
| Archive | Race Discrimination | (1) MR M J ELDRIDGE (2) BARBICAN CAR HIRE LTD | MR L ZHANG | HIS HONOUR JUDGE PETER CLARK | 09/03/2001 |
| Search | Contract of Employmen | MR B DIXON | LONDON BOROUGH OF HACKNEY | HIS HONOUR JUDGE J ALTMAN | 09/03/2001 |

*Employment Law Courses*
http://www.jsb.uk.com
The Janner, Secher, Bennison group offers courses, consulting research and publishing services on employment law. It has a wide-ranging portfolio of updating and new courses on regulation and issue s in employment law.

*Equal Opportunities Commission*
http://www.eoc.org.uk
The EOC site explains its role and powers, and contains guidance on how to eliminate gender discrimination. It also offers a useful set of fact sheets, information on latest campaigns, as well as a research digest.

*European Trade Union Confederation*
http://www.etuc.org
The ETUC is the European trade union movement's EU 'social partner' body, negotiating on behalf of workers across the EU. This site gives useful up-to-date information about EU regulations at work and future developments.

*Health and Safety Executive*
http://www.open.gov.uk/hse/hsehome.htm
The Health and Safety Executive's site gives information on current health and safety laws. It has very good EU documents and commentaries.

*Low Pay Commission*
http://www.dti.gov.uk/lowpay
The site of the Low Pay Commission contains some useful data on the national minimum wage.

*Trades Union Congress*
http://www.tuc.org.uk
This is the official site of the Trades Union Congress (TUC), the employees' representative body. It provides information to more than 70 unions and over 6.7 million members. It gives information on rights, and useful contacts. This is an invaluable source of up-to-date information and discussion on trade union law, of value to any employment lawyer.

## Employment law research sites

*Emplaw*
http://www.emplaw.co.uk
This is a dedicated UK employment law internet site. It includes a free area and a professional area, the latter being updated about every three weeks (except during law vacations). The site has attracted over 35,000 hits since it was set up in 1997. More than 1,200 free pages of basic employment law information are available here. There is also an interactive UK map for locating solicitors with employment law expertise. Law firms with employment law capability are eligible for free email links on application.

# Employment, family & social welfare law ...........................

Fig. 28. Emplaw.

*IRS*
http://www.irseclipse.co.uk
The IRS group offers research and law reporting services. This site is particularly useful for the latest employment news and for access to the Industrial Relations Law Reports.

*Incomes Data Services*
http://www.incomesdata.co.uk
IDS is a specialist employment law company which provides information and research on employment law matters. Its services cover:

Pay and labour market data
Employment law
HR topics
Management pay
Pensions
Employment Europe
Research reports
International documents
Other general statistical data relevant to employment law

## Family law

Many of the law research sites given in Part One of this guide cover how to access family law links. However, below are some of the key web sites with accessible information:

*Family Law Consortium*
http://www.tflc.co.uk
The Family Law Consortium was created in 1995 and combines the

experience and specialisation of three of England's top family law solicitors with two leading non-lawyer mediators and counsellors. It is probably England's first practice to bring together lawyers, mediators and counsellors. This site provides articles, updates and links.

*Family Mediators Association*
http://www.familymediators.co.uk
As family law practitioners will be aware, under the provisions of the 1996 Family Law Act, mediation in family law cases in relation to divorce has become a prerequisite stage. Subsequently, mediators have been appointed. This is the site of the Family Mediators Association which offers advice on their function and discussion pages on current controversial topics facing mediators.

Fig. 29. The Family Mediators Association.

*Jordans Family Law*
http://www.familylaw.co.uk
Jordans offers a free online service updated weekly, containing summaries of the latest cases, legislation and practice developments. There is also a discussion group and a useful set of links.

*Lord Chancellor's Department*
http://www.open.gov.uk/lcd/
As noted in previous chapters, this Lord Chancellor's Department site provides a section on family matters and links to the Child Support Agency:

http://www.dss.gov.uk/csa/

*Social Security and Child Support Commissioners*
http://www.hywels.demon.co.uk/commrs/
This is the site of the Social Security and Child Support Commissioners. It provides case law coverage and the latest news on Family Working

# Employment, family & social welfare law ...........................

Tax Credit and other benefits relevant to family law practice, as well as pensions. In addition, it covers Child Support (see below).

### Social security law

*Social Security & Child Support Commissioners*
http://www.hywels.demon.co.uk/commrs
This is a site for social welfare lawyers, and a primary source of information on recent Commissioners' decisions. It includes a list of Commissioners, and a description of their work, case law, and up-to-date interpretation and guidance on social security legislation. This is a particularly useful site, given the closure of the Central Adjudication Services (www.cas.gov.uk) site as of 26 November 1999, where you could find Neligan's Digest of Commissioners' Decisions. The Commissioners' site is also available in the Welsh language.

Fig. 30. The Social Security Commissioners.

Bookmarks Location: http://www.hywels.demon.co.uk/commrs/decns.htm What's Relate

# The Social Security and Child Support Commissioners

## Commissioners' Decisions on the Internet

### Index Page - Subject Index 1995-2001

*last updated 22 March 2001*

Now in **5**th continuous year! These pages first went live on 16 November 1996. Only ever intended as a short term demonstration of the usefulness of this medium, they continue in the hope that a full up to date coverage from the Court Service will one day make them obsolete.

This page is the starting point for the Subject Index 1995-2001. It also contains notes on some Current appeals and events (including what is new on this site), the numbering and reporting of decisions, how to get hold of decisions not on the Net, the Copyright Notice, and some other links of

### Pressure groups and networks

*Amnesty International*
http://www.oneworld.org/amnesty
This is the home page of Amnesty International, the high-profile human rights campaigning organisation. It was launched in 1961 by a British lawyer called Peter Benenson, after he had read about two Portuguese students sentenced to seven years' imprisonment for raising their glasses in a toast to freedom. This is a substantial web site with numerous links, news features and reports.

*Campaign Against Censorship of the Internet*
http://www.liberty.org.uk/cacib
The Campaign Against Censorship of the Internet in Britain campaigns

against all forms of censorship, for privacy and the right to use strong encryption.

*EmuNet*
http://www.euro.emu.co.uk
EmuNet offers practical information, commentary, and analysis of the UK and the Euro.

*European Movement*
http://www.euromove.org.uk
The European Movement's site. As Britain's pro-European organisation; campaigns to ensure that the benefits of membership are understood by the public.

*Institute for Citizenship Studies*
http://www.citizen.org.uk
Developed by the UK Government, the Institute for Citizenship works directly with teachers, students and Local Education Authorities to develop, pilot and evaluate resources that support the teaching and learning of citizenship. Citizenship is now part of the National Curriculum.

*Liberty*
http://www.liberty-human-rights.org.uk
Liberty, formerly known as the National Council for Civil Liberties, is the leading UK organisation for the defence of civil rights.

Fig. 31. The web site of the watchdog organisation Liberty.

*Taking Liberties*
http://www.tim1.demon.co.uk
Taking Liberties is a UK civil liberties site. It provides some useful news,

articles, legal information, and reports on demos, campaigns, miscarriages of justice and more.

*United Nations Association*
http://www.oneworld.org/UNA_UK
The United Nations Association site is worth exploring for news and comment on the work of the UN and its agencies. You will find comment on UK government attitudes and policies on international affairs, overseas aid and more.

# 8 Company/commercial and property law

In this chapter we will explore:

▶ *company law sources*
▶ *property law sources*
▶ *taxation*
▶ *insolvency*

. . . . . . . . . . . . . . . . . . . . . . . . . . . . . . . . . . . . . . . . . . . . . . . . . . . .

## Company law sources

*Centre for the Study of Business Law & Practice*
http://www.leeds.ac.uk/law/lawcfblp/cfblp.htm
This Leeds University Centre is one of the Department's three Research Centres. It exists to promote the study of all areas of Business Law, understood as the legal rules which regulate any form of business activity. It seeks to promote both theoretical and applied (including empirical) research and to develop contacts between the academic world and the worlds of business and legal practice in order to enhance mutual understanding and awareness. The results of its work are disseminated by publishing monographs, articles and pamphlets as well as by holding seminars with both in-house and outside speakers.

*Companies House*
http://www.companies-house.gov.uk
Companies House holds information on over 1.5 million registered companies and receives over 5 million documents every year. The Companies House Direct service provides a fast, accurate and inexpensive way of obtaining up-to-date information. Its Windows-based internet-style service enables customers to use a web browser to

Fig. 32. Companies House has developed a very useful online service.

75

access the wide range of information on its public databases, to place orders for microfiche or hard-copy documents, and to download or view online images of documents. The site contains guidance notes, online booklets, information on products and services, forms, and the all important site search and email enquiries. Its digital products and services specifically include:

1. Electronic filing of information.

2. Companies House Direct – company accounts and data at the touch of a button.

3. A monthly CD ROM containing the full index of company names.

4. An annual index of change of name and dissolved companies.

A premium service called Online Image Viewing offers quicker access and allows you to select images of documents held on its database and view either selected pages or the complete document online. The same image-viewing software is needed to view these documents. The Companies House site includes links to its electronic business strategy, annual report and accounts, international advisory services, functions, targets and policies, contact details and complaints, links to other sites, feedback, surveys and electronic bulletin, reports, literature and press releases.

*Company Law Club*
http://www.companylawclub.co.uk
The site offers a regular updating service, including a digest of reported cases, new legislation (including statutory instruments), news and views on company law issues, book notices, new websites; a bulletin board for company law topics, including specific boards for company law reform and students' interests; and a library of the most accessible source of UK company law material available online.

*Company Law Index – Swarbrick*
http://www.swarb.co.uk/lisc/Company.html
This page contains some brief company law case law summaries, written by David Swarbrick with Wrigley Claydon Solicitors. The summaries indicate the area of company law, the Court, series, date, case title, ratio decidendi/analysis, and statutes or references.

*Company Law Review*
http://www.dti.gov.uk/cld/review.htm
In March 1998 the DTI launched a long-term fundamental review of core company law with the aim of developing a simple, modern, efficient and cost effective framework for conducting business activity in Britain. The Steering Group has published a number of consultation documents covering a wide range of issues. Copies of all review consultation documents are available as downloadable PDF files.

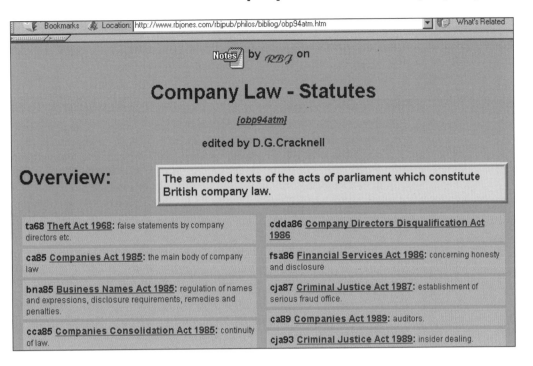

Bookmarks    Location: http://www.rbjones.com/rbjpub/philos/bibliog/obp94atm.htm    ▼ What's Related

Notes by *RBJ* on

# Company Law - Statutes

*[obp94atm]*

edited by D.G.Cracknell

## Overview:

The amended texts of the acts of parliament which constitute British company law.

**ta68 Theft Act 1968:** false statements by company directors etc.

**ca85 Companies Act 1985:** the main body of company law

**bna85 Business Names Act 1985:** regulation of names and expressions, disclosure requirements, remedies and penalties.

**cca85 Companies Consolidation Act 1985:** continuity of law.

**cdda86 Company Directors Disqualification Act 1986**

**fsa86 Financial Services Act 1986:** concerning honesty and disclosure

**cja87 Criminal Justice Act 1987:** establishment of serious fraud office.

**ca89 Companies Act 1989:** auditors.

**cja93 Criminal Justice Act 1989:** insider dealing.

*Company Law Statutes*

http://www.rbjones.com/rbjpub/philos/bibliog/obp94atm.htm

This is an essential site for company lawyers. It offers an overview, and copies of the latest amended texts of the Acts of Parliament which constitute British company law (edited by D. Cracknell).

*Company Law Practice*

http://www.greenslist.com.au/acompanylaw.htm

This site offers guidance to all areas of company law practice. The advice is given by leading silks in company law: Greg Davies QC, Dr John Emmerson QC, John Kaufman QC, Stephen Kaye QC, David Levin QC, Ada Moshinsky QC, Geoffrey Nettle QC and Neil Young QC.

*Company Law Portals*

http://www.cisti.nrc.ca/irc/thesaurus/company.law.html

This site offers links to company law portals, for example commercial law, private law remedies, and bankruptcy.

*European Business Law Review*

http://elj.warwick.ac.uk/juk/journals/eblr.html

The site introduces the *European Business Law Review* which is published by Kluwer Law International in eleven issues per year.

*Hieros Gamos*

http://www.hg.org/commerc.html

This is a substantial US and international law and government portal, with links to: business centre, consumer centre, law students, legal

Fig. 33. Company Law Statutes.

guides, discussion groups, employment, practice areas, law firms, and US court cases.

*Institute of Chartered Secretaries and Administrators*
http://www.icsa.org.uk/isca/

*Intellectual Property*
http://www.intellectual-property.gov.uk
This official UK government site aims to bring you all the answers to your questions and all the resources you need to find your way through the IP jungle of copyright, designs, patents and trade marks. Among the questions discussed are: What is intellectual property or IP? How do I get protection for my idea/material? How will my idea/material benefit from IP? How do I enforce my rights? Do I always need permission to use IP? How do I get permission to use someone's material? What is a domain name? Can I patent computer software?

*International Centre for Commercial Law*
http://www.icclaw.com
ICC Law includes The Legal 500 Series of recommended law firms and lawyers worldwide, a guide to the legal market in over 60 countries covering the UK, Europe, the Middle East, Asia and the US, plus in-depth independent editorial, tables of recommendations and a law firms directory. It also offers a range of UK Company Law articles. It is maintained by Legalease, an independent publishing company.

*International Company and Commercial Law Review*
http://www.smlawpub.co.uk/journal/icclr/
The journal is published by Sweet & Maxwell.

*Northern Ireland Company Registry*
http://www.dedni.gov.uk/registry/index.htm
There are approximately 14,000 companies on the register, filing over 50,000 documents annually. The register includes companies, credit unions and industrial and provident societies. The web site explains the Registry's code of enforcement with links to foreword, terminology, what this code is about, consultation and communication, what we do, what we need from you, further guidance, value for money, independent monitoring, customer care, if you are not satisfied, how you can contact us, and notes for guidance.

*Patent Office and Trademarks*
http://www.patent.gov.uk
The UK Patent Office is responsible for intellectual property (copyright, designs, patents and trade marks) in the UK. The site includes details of its strategy for electronic service delivery and process automation and the European eBusiness project for the intellectual property sector.

*Stationery Office Official Documents*
http://www.official-documents.co.uk
This is a service being developed by The Stationery Office to help internet

Fig. 34. The Patent Office.

users locate official documents, such as the Budget details. It provides access to material published by The Stationery Office and other authoritative bodies.

## Property law sources and practice links

*Edinburgh Solicitors Property Centre*
http://www.espc.co.uk
The site includes some notes on the Scottish legal process. The main headings are: noting interest, closing date, offer and acceptance (missives), examining title deeds, preparing disposition and loan documentation, settlement and date of entry, recording of disposition and standard security, and sending off title deeds and searches.

*EGi Property Law Service*
http://www.propertylaw.co.uk
This is the substantial web site of the weekly magazine, *Estates Gazette* (Estates Gazette Interactive). It provides authoritative updates and articles on property case law and regulations, and other legal developments. As a subscriber to EGi you can get property news updated hourly, summaries of the latest deals, ratings lists, a who's who, legal reports and more from around £400. You can take out a two-week free trial. The site is a service of Reed Business Information.

*HM Land Registry*
http://www.landreg.gov.uk
The site provides information about the work of the Land Registry, forms for use in lodging applications, and various publications offering guidance on a range of subjects. Many documents available on this site are available in Adobe PDF format. To view these documents you will need the Adobe Acrobat PDF viewer (version 3.0 or later). If you do not have

# Company/commercial and property law ............................

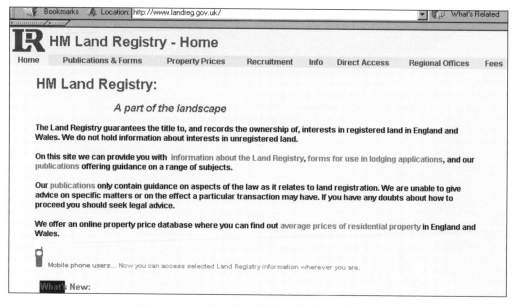

**LR** **HM Land Registry - Home**

Home    Publications & Forms    Property Prices    Recruitment    Info    Direct Access    Regional Offices    Fees

## HM Land Registry:

### A part of the landscape

The Land Registry guarantees the title to, and records the ownership of, interests in registered land in England and Wales. We do not hold information about interests in unregistered land.

On this site we can provide you with information about the Land Registry, forms for use in lodging applications, and our publications offering guidance on a range of subjects.

Our publications only contain guidance on aspects of the law as it relates to land registration. We are unable to give advice on specific matters or on the effect a particular transaction may have. If you have any doubts about how to proceed you should seek legal advice.

We offer an online property price database where you can find out average prices of residential property in England and Wales.

Mobile phone users... Now you can access selected Land Registry information wherever you are.

What's New:

Fig. 35. The Land Registry.

this, you can download it free of charge from here. There is also an online property price database where you can find out average prices of residential property in England and Wales.

▶ Mobile phone users can now access selected Land Registry information from any location. This includes: obtaining residential property price data down to postcode sector level, obtaining contact details for Land Registry regional offices, finding out which of these regional offices deals with property in your area, and calculating Land Registry fees for most standard applications. This is a free service. You only pay your operator for the cost of a call.

*Party Walls*
http://www.surveying.salford.ac.uk/partywall
Salford University: Party Wall Resources site.

*Registers of Scotland*
http://www.open.gov.uk/ros/roshome.htm
These are the Registers of Scotland for Scottish conveyancers.

*Valuation Office Agency*
http://www.voa.gov.uk
This government office is responsible for providing valuations for land and business to a variety of public and private sector customers. Although an agency of the Inland Revenue it has its own web site here.

## Taxation

*Chartered Institute of Taxation*
http://www.tax.org.uk
The aim of this web site is to provide comprehensive, current tax

information to members, students, tax professionals and those seeking advice.

*HM Customs and Excise Home Page*
http://www.hmce.gov.uk
This site includes all its publications together with advice and information on value added tax (VAT).

*Inland Revenue*
http://www.inlandrevenue.gov.uk
The Inland Revenue is responsible, under the overall direction of Treasury Ministers, for the efficient administration of income tax, tax credits, corporation tax, capital gains tax, petroleum revenue tax, inheritance tax, national insurance contributions, and stamp duties. This developing and well-organised web site includes a large number of helpful links for tax professionals.

Fig. 36. The web site of the Inland Revenue.

*Tax-News*
http://www.tax-news.com
This independent UK-based site offers articles on offshore tax, and ecommerce, legal, politcal, and economic news relating to taxes.

*Taxup*
http://www.taxup.com
This is a detailed independent guide to worldwide tax rates, plus business and legal news for professionals and investors.

# Company/commercial and property law ....................................

*Web Directory: UK Taxation Directory*
http://www.uktax.demon.co.uk
Here is a useful portal site of UK taxation resources on the internet, plus an email directory of UK tax professionals.

## Insolvency

*Insolvency*
http://www.insolvency.co.uk/insolco.htm
The Insolvency web site began life in 1996 and has developed into a major UK online resource. Its aims are to promote the UK insolvency profession, to summarise all internet resources regarding insolvency and bankruptcy on one site, to carry official announcements regarding insolvency, to make it approachable and easy for the public to find information about insolvency, and for the insolvency professional to promote his business and to find information relevant to his profession on the internet. The site includes links to the home pages of insolvency practitioners, insolvency courses, and several professional bodies specialising in insolvency.

*Insolvency Practitioners Association*
http://www.ipa.uk.com
Founded in 1961, the IPA is the only professional body whose membership comprises solely of insolvency practitioners and who, in the main, act as trustees in bankruptcy, nominees and supervisors of voluntary arrangements, liquidators, administrators and administrative receivers of companies.

Fig. 37. The Insolvency Practitioners Association.

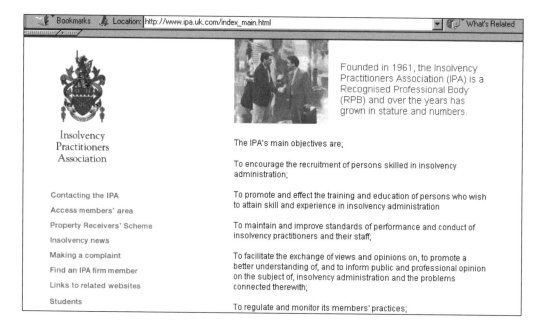

Bookmarks   Location: http://www.ipa.uk.com/index_main.html    What's Related

Insolvency Practitioners Association

Contacting the IPA
Access members' area
Property Receivers' Scheme
Insolvency news
Making a complaint
Find an IPA firm member
Links to related websites
Students

Founded in 1961, the Insolvency Practitioners Association (IPA) is a Recognised Professional Body (RPB) and over the years has grown in stature and numbers.

The IPA's main objectives are;

To encourage the recruitment of persons skilled in insolvency administration;

To promote and effect the training and education of persons who wish to attain skill and experience in insolvency administration

To maintain and improve standards of performance and conduct of insolvency practitioners and their staff;

To facilitate the exchange of views and opinions on, to promote a better understanding of, and to inform public and professional opinion on the subject of, insolvency administration and the problems connected therewith;

To regulate and monitor its members' practices;

*Society of Practitioners of Insolvency*
http://www.spi.org.uk
This is the web site of the Association of Business Recovery professionals.

## More Internet Handbooks to help you

▶ *Homes & Property on the Internet* by Philip Harrison. A guide to thousands of top web sites for buyers, sellers, owners, tenants, sharers, holidaymakers and property professionals

A free illustrated catalogue is available from the publishers (see back cover for details).

# 9 Arbitration & expert witnesses

In this chapter we provide sites on:

▶ *dispute resolution*
▶ *expert witnesses*

. . . . . . . . . . . . . . . . . . . . . . . . . . . . . . . . . . . . . . . . . . . . . . . . . . . . . . . . . . . . . . . . . . . . . .

## Dispute resolution

Since the introduction of the Woolf Reforms, there have been more intense talks about the usage of 'alternative dispute resolution', the so-called methods of ADR: conciliation, mediation and arbitration. As some practitioners are aware, ADR does already exist in some areas of practice. For examples, mediation is currently operated under the Family Law Act 1996 in terms of divorce proceedings, and arbitration, which already exists in employment law matters, pre-Employment Tribunal hearings is to be extended under the 1998 Employment Rights (Disputes Resolution) Act.

Given this growing interest in ADR, we list below some useful sites:

*Adjudication Society*
http://www.adjudication.org
This is a not-for-profit Society formed to promote the resolution of construction disputes by means of adjudication

*Adjudication UK*
http://www.adjudication.co.uk
This organisation offers adjudication services and information including for the construction, telecommunications and security industries. The site contains extensive information on adjudication, a glossary of terms, past cases, legislation links, and news articles and papers.

*Advisory, Conciliation and Arbitration Service*
http://www.acas.org.uk
ACAS has an excellent site covering the latest information on ADR, current statistical data, membership of its Council and other information on settling disputes. For the latest information on unfair dismissal ADR (in force from May 2001) see: http://www.acas.org.uk/arbitration.htm

*Alternative Dispute Resolution Group*
http://www.adrgroup.co.uk
The ADR Group was founded in 1989 and is a specialist mediation provider. Our solicitor mediators have undergone intensive training in mediation and negotiation techniques. Using only solicitors ensures a knowledge of related legal matters. ADR Group regularly arranges mediations in disputes relating to banking, insurance, contract, probate, financial services, contract disputes, as well as medical negligence and personal injury, and offers training in mediation awareness for profes-

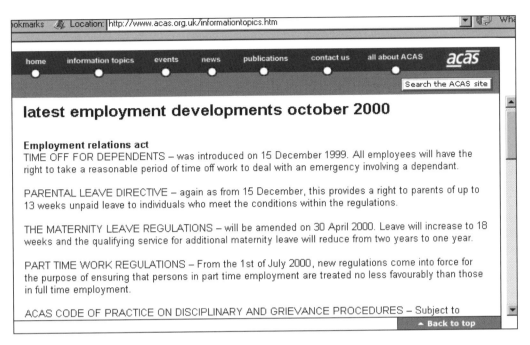

Fig. 38. ACAS.

sionals and corporate bodies, as well as case selection for mediation and confidential advice to disputants. There is a list of firms of solicitors offering mediation services and also a Frequently Asked Questions (FAQ) section about mediation.

### British and Irish Ombudsman Association
http://www.bioa.org.uk
This is a free service that exists to deal with complaints from ordinary citizens, about public or private sector services. It is intended specifically for British and Irish citizens. The site explains: what is a recognised ombudsman, what are ombudsmen for, what does it cost to use an ombudsman, who are the ombudsmen, when the ombudsman acts, time limits, informal resolution, formal investigation, what the ombudsman does, remedies, exclusions, and differences between the schemes.

Fig. 39. The Ombudsmen.

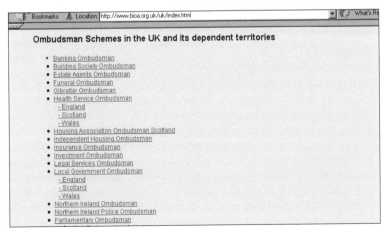

*Centre for Alternative Dispute Resolution*
http://www.cedr.co.uk
The CEDR is a leading international body in the field of Alternative Dispute Resolution, dispute management and conflict prevention. It began in 1990 with the backing of the CBI and aims to be the flagship for raising the understanding, profile and use of alternative dispute resolution, both in the UK and elsewhere.

*Chartered Institute of Arbitrators*
http://www.arbitrators.org
This is a membership organisation aimed at promoting arbitration as the premier means of dispute resolution. Its services include consumer schemes, non-consumer schemes, adjudication, and mediation. A Panel of Commercial and Construction Mediators exists to help people settle any civil dispute without going to court. In addition to developing some tailor-made schemes for commercial bodies, the Institute also runs its own commercial arbitration scheme, and arbitration rules. A list of recommended adjudicators can be obtained from the Institute.

*Click'n'Settle*
http://www.clicknsettle.com
This is an example of a US-based online service designed to allow parties to settle their disputes. Although, primarily aimed at reaching financial settlements, once registered the parties have only 60 days to negotiate and reach a settlement. If a settlement is not achieved, the parties resort to litigation, as in is the norm in any other suit or dispute.

*Delia Venables Legal Resources*
http://www.venables.co.uk/arbitrat.htm
This is a very useful guide to UK arbitration, alternative dispute resolution and mediation online, containing brief descriptions and links to various organisations, practitioners and resources.

*Mediate Net*
http://www.mediate-net.org
The US University of Maryland's site is at the forefront of online mediation offering parties the opportunity to talk and offer confidential bids, in order to settle disputes.

*Mediation UK*
http://www.mediationuk.org.uk/
Mediation UK is a national charity which represents and supports mediation within local communities. Its aim is to enable local people to live together harmoniously by giving them access to mediators, should they need to resolve a dispute. Community mediation can involve anything from resolving conflicts between neighbours or amongst schoolchildren, to mediating between victims of crime and their offenders. Other matters can include workplace disputes, and grievances against public sector service providers such as the health or education services. Mediation UK represents around 500 mediators, mediation services and individuals

interested in conflict resolution issues. Over 170 registered community mediation services currently exist throughout the UK, offering trained mediators to enable parties in dispute to reach mutually acceptable agreements.

▶ Will online ADR happen in the UK? We will have to wait and see.

## Expert witnesses

*Academy of Experts*
http://www.academy-experts.org
The Academy of Experts site gives contact details of experts in a wide-range of areas and specialist knowledge. There is also some information about training.

*Expert Search*
http://www.expertsearch.co.uk
Expert Search (UK) is a growing online directory of experts, expert witnesses and consultants, together with some links and articles. The directory is organized into medical and non-medical categories. In most cases the links are to individual home pages but in other cases they are to corporate sites such as firm, company, hospital to which the individual is attached. The site also includes a directory of medical and non-medical email addresses.

Fig. 40. The Expert Search web site.

*Expert Witness Group*
http://www.expertwitness.co.uk/
Based in Manchester, the Expert Witness Group is another site providing contacts. The Expert Witness/Expert Consultant system is available in a

number of formats. A printed directory and CD ROM are available free of charge to all law firms, law courts and legal departments in the UK. The data includes contact details, qualifications and a concise resume of their experiences and expertise.

*UK Register of Expert Witnesses.*
http://www.greatbritain.co.uk/experts/
This site offers experts the opportunity to register on a UK Internet Register of Expert Witnesses. You can search the register by experience, qualifications and areas of expertise. These include: accident investigation, alcohol and drug abuse, arbitration, architecture, commercial litigation, construction, criminal, dentistry, equestrian, engineering, finance, food science and technology, fuel and energy, forensic, intellectual property, IT, land litigation, matrimonial, medical accidents, medical negligence, mortgage lending, motoring, nursing, care, obstetrics and gynaecology, personal injury, rehabilitation, professional negligence, psychology, sporting injuries and trichology.

# 10 A law directory

**In this chapter we explore some key web sites for:**

▶ *law firms: solicitors*
▶ *law firms: barristers' chambers*
▶ *law networks*

. . . . . . . . . . . . . . . . . . . . . . . . . . . . . . . . . . . . . . . . . . . . . . . . . . . . . . . . . .

## Law firms: solicitors

It would be impossible to list all UK law firms with web sites, so apologies if a particular firm has been missed out. Here is a selection of some of the better known ones:

*Addleshaw Booth & Co*
http://www.addleshaw.booth.co.uk
Addleshaw Booth & Co acts for 36 of the FTSE 250 companies and 42 of *The Times* top 200 quoted companies. Its clients include 3i plc, Airtours, British Aerospace, British Vita, BT, the Ministry of Defence, Railtrack, Trinity International Holdings and AAH. It has around 100 partners, a further 180 lawyers and more than 200 other fee-earners.

*Allen & Overy*
http://www.allenovery.com
http://www.newchange.com
Founded in 1930, Allen & Overy is a premier London-based international law firm with 268 partners and over 3,000 staff working in 23 major centres worldwide.

Fig. 41. Allen & Overy.

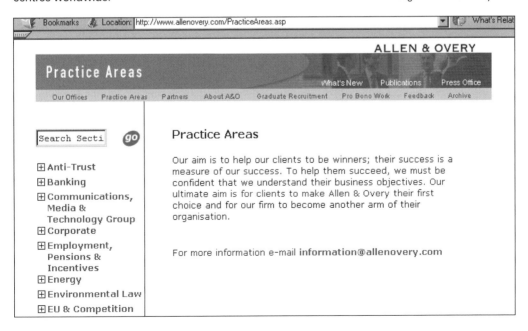

# A law directory .........................................................................

*Ashurst Morris Crisp*
http://www.ashursts.co.uk
Ashursts has been providing legal services for more than 175 years. It recently ranked third in a survey of UK law firms with the highest number of clients listed on the London Stock Exchange. The site contains details of its practice areas, recruitment and publications.

*Baker and McKenzie,*
http://www.bakernet.com
Founded in 1949 Baker and McKenzie is a City of London law firm of over 170 lawyers offering a broad range of services. The firm offers access to its library services and various commercial and legal databases, and internal and external communication through its proprietary Baker-Net email and other networks.

*Barlow Lyde & Gilbert*
http://www.blg.co.uk
With over 70 partners, the firm advises corporate organisations, government bodies, financial and other institutions in all spheres of business activity, from its offices in the City of London Hong Kong, and at Lloyd's. It is well known for its work in litigation and other forms of dispute resolution. The firm offers around 15 training contracts each year.

*Beachcroft Wansbroughs*
http://www.vaudreys.com/
With an annual income of more than £65m, the firm's services are based upon specific client market sectors, mainly in the commercial, health and insurance arenas.

*Berrymans Lace Mawer*
http://www.blm-law.com
The firm has what may be the largest insurance litigation practice in the UK. Over 80 per cent of its work involves advising the insurance market and the firm has one of the UK's largest personal injury practices. It has branches in Birmingham, Leeds, Liverpool, London, Manchester, Southampton and Dubai, and a staff of more than 700 worldwide.

*S J Berwin & Co*
http://www.sjberwin.com
Founded in 1982, S J Berwin & Co acts for clients from major multinational business corporations and financial institutions to high-net-worth individuals. The firm has a number of leading entrepreneurial business clients. It maintains offices in London, Brussels and Frankfurt, and has earnings of around £55m a year.

*Berwin Leighton*
http://www.berwinleighton.com
http://www.t@xand legal.com
Berwin Leighton is a London-based law firm with a recognised expertise in property, finance and corporate law.

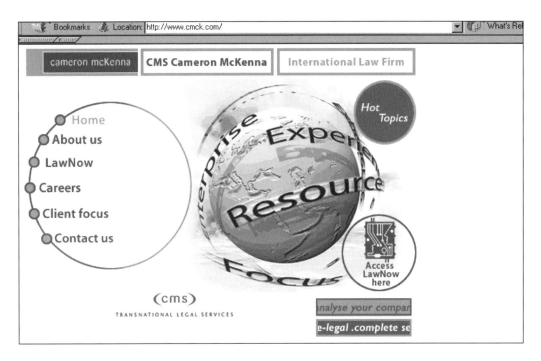

Fig. 42. Cameron McKenna.

*Cameron McKenna*
http://www.cmh.co.uk
http://www.cmck.com
Cameron McKenna has joined forces with five other top European law firms to create CMS, a transnational legal services organisation. The group has 31 offices in 19 jurisdictions in Europe, the CIS, Asia-Pacific and North America and is committed to providing clients with integrated, seamless services. See also its legal updating service at:

http://www.cmck.com

*Clifford Chance*
http://www.CliffordChance.com
http://www.nextlaw.com
Over the years, Clifford Chance has grown into an international, multi-jurisdictional law firm handling all aspects of business and finance, and today grossing some £400m a year in fees. In January 2000 it merged with Rogers & Wells LLP and Pünder, Volhard, Weber & Axster to create Clifford Chance LLP, an integrated global law firm designed to meet the needs of businesses operating in the international market. It is one of the largest law firms in the world with over 3,000 legal advisers

*Clyde & Co*
http://www.clydeco.com
The site includes legal opinions on current world events. Company background and a directory of more than 100 partners, consultants and senior associates can be found here. There are interactive elements, a

regular magazine section and some online archives. Students considering a legal career can check out background information and contact details in its careers section. There is also a useful set of links to online legal, financial, and information resources.

### Davies Arnold Cooper
http://www.dac.co.uk
Established in 1927, the firm is active in the insurance, financial services, construction, commercial property, pharmaceutical, healthcare and retail industries. It has 50 partners and over 430 staff, with offices in London, Manchester, Newcastle, and Madrid. Its web site is offered as an information resource, with sections highlighting key developments updated regularly. A keyword search helps you find what you want quickly and easily.

### Denton Hall
http://www.dentonhall.com
http://www.dentonwildesapte.com
Denton Hall (Denton Wilde Sapte) is a prominent general service business law firm with offices around the world. It offers a comprehensive range of commercial legal advice and is strong in banking and finance, energy and infrastructure, media and technology, property, retail and aviation. The firm is a founder member of Denton International which, with Denton Wilde Sapte, has 33 offices in 21 jurisdictions around the world.

### Dibb Lupton Alsop
http://www.dla-law.co.uk
Dibb Lupton Alsop is one of the UK's top ten law firms. The site features recent news and a news archive, free publications, recruitment, training, ecommerce and other services. All the firm's locations are equipped with video-conferencing facilities, ensuring that clients and partners can speak quickly when necessary.

### Edge Ellison
http://www.edge.co.uk/
The Edge Ellison partnership has corporate, commercial property, and construction and engineering departments, and deals also with litigation, pensions and finance law. The firm employs over 600 people and has an annual fee income of around £35m.

### Eversheds
http://www.eversheds.com
A European law firm, Eversheds has 1,500 legal and business advisers based in 19 locations. Its specialist services encompass business risk services, computer/IT, corporate tax, environment, health and safety, EU and competition law, franchising, insolvency, intellectual property, international public law, licensing, PFI, planning, pensions, private capital and tax matters, and venture capital.

*Field Fisher Waterhouse*
http://www.ffwlaw.com.
This London firm's client base includes commercial and industrial compa-nies, banks and other financial institutions, governments, trade associations, regulatory bodies and professional partnerships. It also acts for a substantial number of overseas clients and has good links with China, France, Germany, Italy, Japan, Korea, Scandinavia and the USA.

*D J Freeman*
http://www.cygnet.co.uk/DJFreeman/
This London-based firm specialises in internet and media law. This page offers some useful guidance notes about the legal implications of the internet viewed from a UK perspective.

*Freshfields Bruckhaus Deringer*
http://www.freshfields.com
Freshfields is an old-established international law firm with a network of 30 offices across Europe, Asia and the USA, providing a comprehensive worldwide service to national and multinational corporations, financial institutions and governments. A market leader in international transac-tions, the firm also has a top domestic practice in many countries.

*Gouldens*
http://www.gouldens.com
With earnings of around £28m, Gouldens is a leading corporate firm based in the City of London. Its specialist groups cover areas such as cor-porate tax, international and personal tax planning, environment, IP, IT, employment, employee benefits and pensions, regulatory matters, fraud and white collar crime. Languages spoken include Dutch, French, German, Greek, Hebrew, Italian, Japanese, Romanian, Russian, Spanish, Welsh and Czech.

*Hammond Suddards*
http://www.hammondsuddards.com
http://www.hammondsuddardsedge.com
Hammond Suddards acts for public and large private companies, banks, building societies, insurance companies and a wide range of financial and other institutions.

*Herbert Smith*
http://www.herbertsmith.com
Founded in 1882, Herbert Smith has developed into a premier interna-tional law firm operating from the City of London, Brussels, Paris, Bangkok, Hong Kong and Singapore. It employs over 725 lawyers and another 700 support staff. It grosses over £140m in fees each year. Its areas of specialism include: administrative and public law, banking, civil fraud, construction, defamation, employment, energy, environment, infor-mation technology, insurance and reinsurance, intellectual property, public and private international law, professional indemnity, regulatory and compliance cases, and sport.

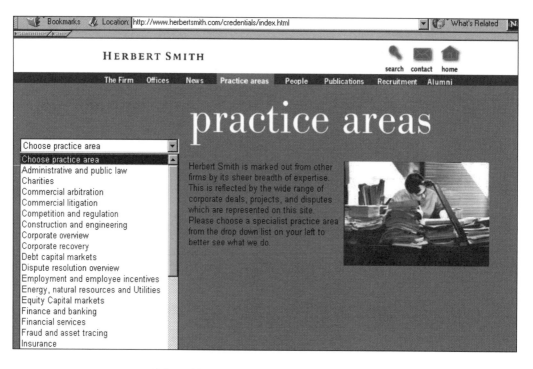

Fig. 43. Herbert Smith.

*Holman Fenwick & Willan*
email@hfw.co.uk
Founded in 1883, HF&W is an international law firm and specialist in maritime transportation, insurance, reinsurance and trade. The firm is a leader in the field of commercial litigation and arbitration and also offers comprehensive commercial and financial advice. It has a network of offices covering London, Paris, Rouen, Nantes, Piraeus, Hong Kong, Shanghai and Singapore.

*Ince*
http://www.ince.co.uk
Ince specialises in maritime and insurance law, and has been involved in some major cases of maritime disasters and environmental pollution. It operates a 24-hour emergency response service 365 days a year in respect of maritime, aviation and energy related casualties. It handles cases covering all aspects of international trade, from its offices in the City of London, Hong Kong, Singapore, and Piraeus.

*Irwin Mitchell*
http://www.irwinmitchell.co.uk
Established over 80 years ago, Sheffield-based Irwin Mitchell specialises in general commercial and litigation work, housing association and public sector work, personal injury, medical negligence and product liability work, and work for private clients. It has 74 partners and over 1,000 staff.

*Lawrence Graham*
http://www.lawgram.com
The 400-strong firm is based in London and its business is organised into four main practice areas: commercial property, corporate/commercial, litigation, and tax and financial management. The commercial property department is the largest in the firm. The firm also has an office in the Ukraine where it has had clients since the 1920s.

*Linklaters*
http://www.linklaters.com
http://www.blueflag.com
Established more than 150 years ago, Linklaters is generally regarded as one of the world's premier global law firms, operating from the UK and major financial centres around the world. The firm offers a full range of legal services in corporate work, international finance, commercial property, litigation, IP, technology, communications and tax. It is a member of Linklaters & Alliance which comprises five of Europe's leading law firms

*Lovell White Durrant*
http://www.lovellwhitedurrant.com
Lovell White Durrant is a European-based international law firm operating worldwide from offices in London, Chicago, New York, Paris, Brussels, Prague, Ho Chi Minh City, Hong Kong, Beijing and Tokyo.

*Macfarlanes*
http://www.macfarlanes.com
The partnership works with clients in industrial and commercial sectors. Its main areas of practice are company commercial and banking, property, litigation, and tax and financial planning. It has 54 partners and a staff of around 420. It publishes a range of practice notes, newsletters, and guidance notes for clients.

*Masons*
http://www.masons.com
http://www.out-law.com
Established over 50 years ago, Masons' London operation is supported by a regional network of offices in Leeds, Manchester, Bristol and Glasgow. International matters are handled by Masons' offices in Brussels, Dublin, Hong Kong, Guangzhou (China) and Singapore. The firm is noted for its services to the computer, infrastructure, and engineering and construction industries.

*Merriman White*
http://www.merrimanwhite.co.uk
This London firm specialises in medical, injury, patents, consumer, company and commercial law. They say: 'We have been established since 1740 and based in King's Bench Walk from that time.' Its web site offers a 'free assessment of your personal injury claim'.

### Morgan Cole
http://www.morgan-cole.com/
Morgan Cole is located along the M4 corridor. It has a fee income in excess of £30m, and seven offices in London, the Thames Valley and South Wales providing a service to commercial clients across the UK.

### Nabarro Nathanson
http://www.nabarro.com/
This leading firm has more than 100 partners and approximately 350 other lawyers working in offices in London, Reading and Sheffield, as well as Brussels where it has a specialist EU and competition law unit. The site includes illustrated partner profiles.

Fig. 44. Nabarro Nathanson.

### Norton Rose
http://www.nortonrose.com
Norton Rose is a major international law firm with its principal office in the City of London and a worldwide network of offices from Athens to Bangkok. It acts for banks and other financial institutions, international businesses, major public and private companies, government departments and sovereign states. The company is particularly active in corporate finance, debt, asset and project finance, banking and capital markets, and company and commercial law. The web site includes a section of career opportunities, and a legal resources room.

### Olswang
http://www.olswang.co.uk
http://www.olswang.com
Olswang provides corporate, commercial, property and litigation advice to the media, communications, entertainment and technology sectors in the UK and overseas. Formed in 1981, it now has 47 partners, 189 lawyers, and 222 support staff. It operates a 'dress down Friday' policy.

### Pannone & Partners
http://www.pannone.com
A Manchester-based law firm.

*Pinsent Curtis*
http://www.pinsents.com
The firm combines a strong City of London operation with major offices in the principal business centres of the UK. It has around 130 partners and 800 staff operating from offices in London, Birmingham, Leeds and Brussels. The web site includes links to meet the partners, and recruitment.

*Richards Butler*
http://www.richardsbutler.com
With over 1,000 staff worldwide, the London-based firm acts mainly for larger international clients concerned with banking and financial services; commodity trading; insurance; media, entertainment and leisure; information technology and telecommunications; shipping; and property. More than half its work has an international dimension.

*Rowe and Maw*
http://www.roweandmaw.co.uk
Founded over 100 years ago, Rowe & Maw is one of the UK's leading commercial law firms, based in the City of London. It also advise clients internationally, either through its EU and competition law office in Brussels or through a well established network of contacts,

*Shoosmiths*
http://www.shoosmiths.co.uk
The practice of this regional firm comprises six main sectors: business services, property services, financial institutions, banking, personal injury, and private client. Its gross fee income is around £36m, and it has a staff of around 1,000 people.

*Simmons and Simmons*
http://www.elexica.com
Simmons and Simmons, the international law firm, offers free internet access for students and lawyers. This site aspires to build an online legal community for its clients. It offers not only newsletters, online checklists and links, but also discussion forums. It has offices in Europe, Asia, and the United States.

*Slaughter & May*
http://www.slaughterandmay.com
Slaughter and May is a leading and old-established English law firm with a very large international corporate, commercial and financial practice. It has a worldwide staff of over 1,200 including some 600 lawyers. There is a section on careers which includes a brief preview of the firm and its practice, details of career opportunities, and vacation schemes, and how to make an application to join the firm. You can also apply online for a graduate opportunities brochure.

# A law directory ......................................................

Fig. 45. Slaughter & May.

*Stephenson Harwood*
http://www.StephensonHarwood.com
The firm specialises in corporate finance, banking, property, and a high-profile litigation and arbitration practice. It is one of the few leading City of London law firms that still undertakes private client, family and matrimonial work.

*Taylor Joynson Garrett*
http://www.tjg.co.uk
Taylor Joynson Garrett is a prominent City of London law firm. It produces regular updates on various legal issues which can be accessed via this web site. It is ranked among the top thirty law firms in London, having over 450 staff, 240 lawyers and 82 partners.

Fig. 46. Taylor Joynson Garrett.

*Theodore Goddard*
http://www.theogoddard.com
Founded in 1902, Theodore Goddard is today a premier City of London-based firm with many famous clients. It advises on all aspects of business-related law, in particular banking, finance, music, broadcasting, theatre, film and television, property, publishing, and employment. They say that their modern approach is backed by a solid investment in information technology, highly effective communications systems and training at all levels.

*Thompsons*
http://www.thompsons.law.co.uk
Since 1921, Thompsons has grown into one of the largest personal injury practices in the UK. It has a national network of 14 offices. The firm only acts for claimants' personal injury work and for employees in employment and criminal matters. It regularly secures more than £100,000 in compensation amounts for clients. The firm also undertakes conditional fee work.

*Titmuss Sainer Dechert*
http://www.titmuss-sainer-dechert.com
The firm serves commercial, industrial, property, financial, and individual clients in a range of specialties, including retail, litigation, and financial services.

*Travers Smith Braithwaite*
http://www.traverssmith.co.uk
With over 160 lawyers, London-based Travers Smith Braithwaite is one of the UK's leading corporate, financial and commercial law firms. The impressively fast-loading site includes details of professional and graduate recruitment. You can click on links to read three case studies involving trainee solicitors at the firm.

*Watson, Farley & Williams*
http://www.wfw.com/
Founded in 1982, this is an international commercial law firm specialising in shipping and aircraft finance, litigation, and general corporate law. Based in the City of London, it has offices worldwide. Its staff can advise on English, French, Russian, New York and US federal laws.

*Wragge & Co*
http://www.wragge.co.uk/
Birmingham-based Wragge & Co provides a comprehensive service for major companies, public authorities and financial institutions, in the UK and overseas, including over 165 listed companies. About a fifth of its work is international. Its fee income amounts to some £50m and its major clients include BA, PowerGen, Severn Trent, Cadbury Schweppes, and AT&T.

## Law firms: barristers chambers

This is a cross-section of barristers' chambers which have developed an online presence. The chambers are based both inside and outside London, and cover a variety of legal disciplines.

*1 Mitre Court Buildings*
http://www.1mitrecourt.com/
This is a specialist set of chambers in which all members practise exclusively in the field of family law. They offer a range of services covering financial relief, care proceedings, adoption, child abduction and more. There are currently seven QCs and 23 junior barristers. Among former members of chambers are Lord Simon of Glaisdale and Lady Justice Butler-Sloss. They say: 'Most members of Chambers have their own personal computers and can provide documents on disk or by email. All members of Chambers belong to the Family Law Bar Association.'

*One King's Bench Walk*
http://www.1kbw.co.uk
They say: 'We are an established set of chambers with members at all levels of seniority who between them undertake a broad range of work. Many of them contribute to specialist publications: members currently include two editors of Jackson and Davies *Matrimonial Finance and Taxation*, and an author of Hershman and McFarlane's *Children Law and Practice* and two editors of Archbold's *Criminal Pleading, Evidence and Practice*. We have strong specialist groups in family law, criminal law and general common law as well as individual expertise in many other areas of work.'

*No 6 Barristers Chambers*
http://www.no6.co.uk
These are Leeds-based chambers specialising in family, chancery and commercial, criminal, personal injury, and professional negligence law. The site includes detailed barristers' profiles, linked to their various areas of specialism.

*12 New Square Barristers' Chambers*
http://www.newsquarechambers.co.uk
The chambers' members specialise in chancery and commercial law. They say: 'This new set is now one of the largest in Lincoln's Inn, offering the services of 9 silks and 35 junior counsel, with skills covering the full range of chancery and commercial practice at every level of seniority.' The site includes links to barristers, administration, practice, cases, pupillage, maps and travel, legal news, a day calculator, and search facility.

*24 Old Buildings*
http://www.24oldBuildings.law.co.uk
This set of Chancery Chambers was formed over 25 years ago. They say: 'Since then, Chambers has developed to reflect the changes that have taken place in the Chancery field and it now offers the specialist expertise required for a wide range of commercial and equity disputes and pro-

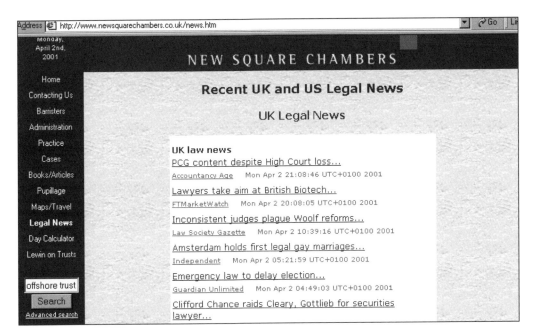

Address http://www.newsquarechambers.co.uk/news.htm  ▼  Go  Li

Monday,
April 2nd,
2001

NEW SQUARE CHAMBERS

Home
Contacting Us
Barristers
Administration
Practice
Cases
Books/Articles
Pupillage
Maps/Travel
**Legal News**
Day Calculator
Lewin on Trusts

offshore trust
Search
Advanced search

## Recent UK and US Legal News

### UK Legal News

**UK law news**
PCG content despite High Court loss...
Accountancy Age    Mon Apr 2 21:08:46 UTC+0100 2001

Lawyers take aim at British Biotech...
FTMarketWatch    Mon Apr 2 20:08:05 UTC+0100 2001

Inconsistent judges plague Woolf reforms...
Law Society Gazette    Mon Apr 2 10:39:16 UTC+0100 2001

Amsterdam holds first legal gay marriages...
Independent    Mon Apr 2 05:21:59 UTC+0100 2001

Emergency law to delay election...
Guardian Unlimited    Mon Apr 2 04:49:03 UTC+0100 2001

Clifford Chance raids Cleary, Gottlieb for securities lawyer...

Fig. 47. New Square Chambers.

blems. Members of Chambers have been involved in some of the most widely reported cases of the last ten years, involving such well-known names as BCCI, Maxwell and Barings.'

*Durham Barristers Chambers*
http://www.durhambarristers.com
They say: 'Established in 1996 by local practitioners, chambers has grown and developed distinct specialisations. Common law matters, crime, civil and commercial law are important areas of work. Planning, environmental and local government law have been specialisations from the outset.' The site includes barristers' profiles.

*Essex Court Chambers*
http://www.essexcourt-chambers.law.co.uk
Its specialist areas include: administrative law and judicial review, agriculture and farming, arbitration, aviation banking, Chinese law, company law and insolvency, conflict of laws, construction and, engineering, commodity transactions, computer law, employment law, energy and utilities law, entertainment and sports law, environmental law, European law, financial services, human rights, injunctions and arrests, insurance and reinsurance, international trade and transport, professional negligence, public international law, public law, sale of goods and product liability, shipping, VAT and excise. The original founding members were Michael Kerr (later Lord Justice Kerr), Robert MacCrindle, Michael Mustill (later Lord Mustill), Anthony Evans (later Lord Justice Evans), and Anthony Diamond (later Judge Diamond), all of whom at some time headed Chambers.

*Guildford Chambers*
http://www.guildfordbarristers.com/
They say: 'Guildford Chambers was established in 1976 as a small annexe of a London set, in the belief that solicitors in the area would welcome the service available from local chambers. That expectation was amply justified and since 1981 Guildford Chambers has been completely independent. In recent years it has expanded rapidly and there are now eighteen barristers, including one Queen's Counsel.'

*Old Square Chambers*
http://www.oldsquarechambers.co.uk/index.html
Its barristers specialise in employment law, environmental law, personal injury and clinical negligence, and product liability law. Detailed members' profiles are included, along with a useful page of legal hyperlinks, and information about pupillage.

*Trinity Chambers*
http://www.trinitychambers.co.uk/
These are barristers' chambers in Newcastle upon Tyne, with principle areas of practice in chancery, commercial, common law, crime, employment, family, and licensing. They say: 'Chambers is the first set north of London, and only the fourth in England and Wales, to gain the British Standard Institutions' accreditation of BarMark, which was ratified by the General Council of the Bar on 10th April 2000.'

## Law networks

*ALeRT UK*
http://www.alertuk.com
ALeRT UK (UK) is a group of law firms dedicated exchanging information.

*LawGroup*
http://www.lawgroup.co.uk
The LawGroup UK is a national network of independent solicitors' firms. It was launched in 1988 to provide a response to the challenge facing independent firms, and since then has continued to grow. Today it comprises over 60 practices throughout the UK with a combined fee income of over £150 million. All have a diverse client range and specific areas of expertise. Member firms can draw on the experience of more than 600 partners and 2,000 staff in over 100 locations. LawGroup says it selects firms who are committed to continual improvement, focusing on client service and quality. Its solicitors are developing new expertise in the fast growing and niche areas of the law, as well as improving their skills and approach to traditional areas of practice.

*LawNet*
http://www.lawnet-uk.com
LawNet provides details on law firms in many locations throughout the United Kingdom, the Republic of Ireland and the Channel Islands. Its online services provide information about the practice of law - using a

Fig. 48. IC Law directories.

lawyer, and the work undertaken. The addresses of relevant authorities, associations and national institutions can also be found by following links on the site.

*International Centre for Commercial Law (ICC Law)*
http://www.icclaw.com/l500/uk.htm
Here you can explore the well-known Legal 500 Series: *The Legal 500, The European Legal 500, The Asia Pacific Legal 500,* and *The Legal 500,* which provides a detailed guide to UK law firms. *The Legal 500* was first published in 1988 and has grown to be the definitive client reference to the UK's commercial law firms. *The Times* newspaper has described *The Legal 500* as 'the bible of the legal business.' The Legal 500 is the most used and most referred to legal directory, with 89 per cent of senior company lawyers using it each year (Gallup). Each year over 20,000 copies are printed and the information is also made available on the internet site (the International Centre for Commercial Law). A team of experienced researchers present reviews of over 80 individual practice areas and assess the strengths of the firms in these fields. The regions are covered in the same way and a section covering the Bar was added in the 1996 edition. The online version of *The Legal 500* is available from this web page.

*Logos*
http://www.logos-eeig.com
Logos is a network of independent law firms in Europe. With one law firm in each of twelve countries of the European Union and contacts in the other three, Logos can assist any business or law firm around the world that needs legal support in Europe.

*National Solicitors Network*
http://www.tnsn.com/
National Solicitors Network is a network of independent solicitors' prac-

tices with over 500 member offices throughout England and Wales which is setting new standards in the provision of high quality, reasonably priced, legal services to private, institutional and corporate clients.

*Lawyers on the Web*
http://www.infolaw.co.uk/ifl/lawyers.htm
Lawyers on the Web is a useful and comprehensive guide to law firms, solicitors and law organisations which have launched internet pages.

## More Internet Handbooks to help you

▶ *Education & Training on the Internet* by Laurel Alexander. An essential reference source for students, teachers, and education providers.

▶ *Where to Find it on the Internet* by Kye Valongo (2nd edition). Your complete guide to search engines, portals, databases, yellow pages and other internet reference tools.

A free illustrated catalogue is available from the publishers (see back cover for details).

# 11 Legal services and practice

**In this chapter we will explore:**

▶ *legal recruitment*
▶ *legal software*
▶ *legal services online*

. . . . . . . . . . . . . . . . . . . . . . . . . . . . . . . . . . . . . . . . . . . . . . . . . . . . . . . . . . . . . . . . . . . .

## Legal recruitment

*Actis Recruitment*
http://www.actisrecruitment.co.uk
Based in Bolton, the firm holds a register of solicitors and legal executives
throughout the UK and deals with positions both in private practice and
in industry. It also recruits company secretaries, practice managers and
development and marketing specialists.

*ASA Law*
http://www.asagroup.co.uk
Founded in 1973 ASA deals both with legal secretarial positions and professional legal recruitment, including contract locums.

*Bygott Biggs*
http://www.bygott-biggs.co.uk
Nottingham-based Bygott Biggs recruits lawyers at all levels, from
newly-qualified individuals to equity partners in every discipline and in
private practice and industry.

*Capital Legal*
http://www.capitallegal.co.uk

*Career Legal*
http://www.careerlegal.co.uk/
This is an independent City of London-based consultancy providing permanent and temporary specialist recruitment services, ranging from
secretarial to legal professional. Its clients range from the largest international law firms to specialist niche market practices.

*Cavendish Boyle*
http://www.cavendish-boyle.com
Established in 1993, the Leeds-based company typically has around 100
vacancies for professional lawyers.

*Chadwick Nott*
http://www.chadwicknott.co.uk
With offices in London and Bristol, Chadwick Nott handles legal
appointments in the UK and as far afield as Cayman Islands, the Carib-
bean, Hong Kong, the Channel Islands and Australasia.

# Legal services and practice .........................................

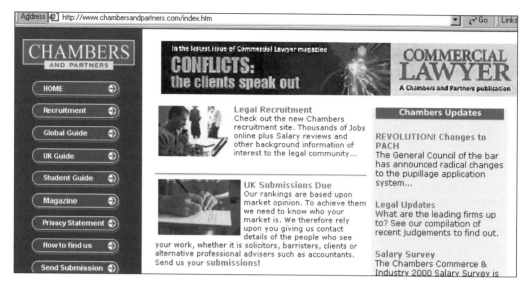

Fig. 49. Chambers Legal Recruitment.

*Chambers & Partners*
http://www.chambersandpartners.com
Based in the City of London, this law recruitment firm is also the publisher of a series of guides to the legal profession (domestic, global and student).

*Chancery Lane Legal Secretaries*
http://www.legal-secretaries.co.uk/
The company provides legal secretaries to the legal profession throughout London.

*Corporatelaw UK*
http://www.corporatelaw-uk.com/
Offers job recruitment services for the legal profession. The web site also includes indicative legal salary information for law jobs and vacancies throughout the UK. This section also includes worldwide legal salary information.

*Crone Corkill Legal*
http://www.cronecorkill.co.uk
The firm often has 40 to 50 vacancies for legal staff, mostly in London.

*EJ Legal*
http://www.ejgroup.co.uk
This kaw recruitment firm was established in 1992 and has offices in Holborn, London. Its client base encompasses niche practices to larger firms in the City and to US firms and multi-office global practices.

*Employment Law, Recruitment and Other Job Related Issues*
http://www.frontier-systems.co.uk/employment_law.htm

### G2 Legal Recruitment Consultancy

http://www.g2legal.com

This firm was established in 1999 and now has offices situated in Manchester and Brighton, serving clients nationwide. It places both permanent and temporary legal professionals including locums, solicitors and legal executives, paralegals, practice managers, office managers and support staff.

### Garfield Robbins

http://www.garfieldrobbins.co.uk

Formed in 1989, the Garfield Robbins Group undertakes legal recruitment in private practice and in-house. It has offices in London, New York, Sydney and Hong Kong. Its business can also be conducted in French, German, Italian, Russian, the Scandinavian languages and Spanish.

### Graham Gill

http://www.grahamgill.com

Based in Kingsway, London, the firm is a search and selection consultancy for the legal profession, specialising in UK and international positions for solicitors, barristers and legal executives in private practice and in-house. It is a founder member of the Legal Section of the Recruitment and Employment Confederation.

### HaysZMB Recruitment Consultants

http://www.zmb.co.uk

HaysZMB is a specialist recruitment consultancy sourcing positions for lawyers, HR, marketing and finance professionals. Its clients include blue chip corporates and financial institutions, top UK and international law firms and public sector bodies. It has offices in London, Manchester, Leeds and Dublin, and is part of Hays Personnel Services Ltd.

### Hemscott Legal

http://www.hemscottlegal.com

The site contains a useful section on recruitment along with a searchable vacancies database, tips on interview techniques and advice on how to prepare a CV.

### Hughes-Castell

http://www.hughescastell.com

Established in 1985, Hughes-Castell recruits qualified lawyers at all levels for both the private practice and in-house sectors. It operates in the London market, where it recruits for the City and the higher profile West End firms, and internationally, with offices in Hong Kong, Australia, New Zealand and affiliates in the US and South Africa.

### Jobs in Law

http://www.jobsinlaw.com

This page is part of a wider online recruitment service based in Royal Leamington Spa, and has occasional vacancies in law.

*Joslin Rowe*
http://www.joslinrowe.com
The London-based firm opened its professional services division in 1999, focusing on the recruitment of finance, HR and marketing professionals for legal practices.

*Kingsmere Legal Recruitment*
http://www.kingsmere.co.uk/
Kingsmere supplies temporary, contract and permanent legal staff covering secretarial, paralegal, legal executives, human resources professionals and office juniors to some of London's top law firms in the City and West End.

*Law Consultants*
http://www.lawcon.co.uk
Law Consultants specialise in the permanent and temporary placement of legal staff from partners/solicitors to legal executives and costs draftspersons in private practice, local government and in-house. The firm is based in Fulbourn, Cambridgeshire.

*Law Society Recruitment*
http://www.recruitment.lawsociety.org.uk

Fig. 50. The Law Society web site has its own online recruitment service.

Under the Law Society umbrella, this organisation operates as a recruitment agency providing an ethical and confidential service to solicitors, legal executives, practice managers, and paralegals.

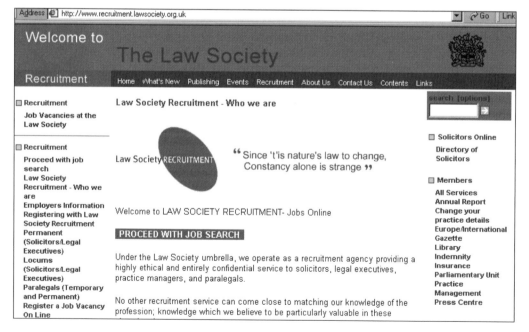

*LPA Legal Recruitment*
http://www.legalrecruitment.co.uk
This is the web site of a London-based legal recruitment agency which

places lawyers at firms throughout the UK and abroad. You can submit your CV online.

*Michael Page Legal*
http://www.michaelpage.co.uk
Established in 1985, Michael Page Legal specialises in the recruitment of legally qualified personnel, sourcing both permanent and temporary/contract staff. Clients include the top 200 UK and prominent US law firms and a large cross section of corporate and banking clients who have in-house legal departments. The firm has offices in London, Birmingham, Bristol, Hong Kong, Paris, Sydney and Melbourne.

*MRI Worldwide*
http://www.mriww-ls.com
Quoted on the New York Stock Exchange, MRI is one of the largest search organisations in the world, with almost 1,000 offices worldwide. Opened in 1996, its UK practice based in Solihull specialises entirely in the placement of solicitors.

*ProLaw*
http://www.prolaw.co.uk
Based in Chancery Lane, London, ProLaw supplies paralegals and locum solicitors to top law firms, local and central government and industry.

*PSD Law Recruitment*
http://www.psd.co.uk/law/
This is the legal services department of a London-based international recruiting firm. It has a good number of opportunities for legal professionals for practice, industry and banking.

*Taylormade Legal Services*
http://www.taylormadelaw.com
The company is based in Banbury, Oxfordshire, and recruits lawyers, legal secretaries, paralegals, cashiers, fee earners and part time personnel.

*The Times newspaper*
http://www.thetimes.co.uk/appointments

*TNTU Electronic Library Resources: Law UK*
http://www.ntu.ac.uk/lis/lawrecruitment.htm
Check out law training and courses and links to other recruitment sites.

*Totally Legal*
http://www.totallylegal.com
This is a specialist recruitment web site for law. You can view law firms' profiles and current vacancies.

Fig. 51. Totally Legal.

## Legal software

### Axiom
http://www.axiombc.co.uk
Axiom is a specialist in financial systems for Scottish legal and commercial sectors. It is a member of the Legal Software Suppliers Association. Built around Client Record Manager, the system's fully relational database, Axiom's Practice Manager software is designed to increase the efficiency, quality and profitability of professional practice.

### City Group
http://www.timeslice.co.uk
The company develops software for solicitors including Lawman2000 which incorporates practice management, legal accounting, case management, billing, and more.

### Compiforce
http://www.compiforce.com
Compiforce offers debt recovery and litigation software for debt collectors, bailiffs, solicitors and enquiry agents.

### Delia Venables Legal Resources
http://www.venables.co.uk/software.htm
This looks to be a very comprehensive and well-organised guide to suppliers of software and IT for solicitors. It is complete with brief descriptions, and links to the web sites of the suppliers.

### Grierson's Legal Office Manager Software
http://www.griersons.com
The software produced by this Newcastle upon Tyne firm provides con-

trol of all files within the practice. This includes instant identification of conflict, cross referencing of client matters, a link to word processing via case data, a date recording process, and the value of case work is immediately available. A series of simple data bases provides information on case loads and fee earning.

*Legal Software Suppliers Association*
http://www.lssa.co.uk
The site contains details of members by name, a code of practice and complaints procedure. The association is based in Stratford upon Avon.

Fig. 42. The Legal Software Suppliers Association.

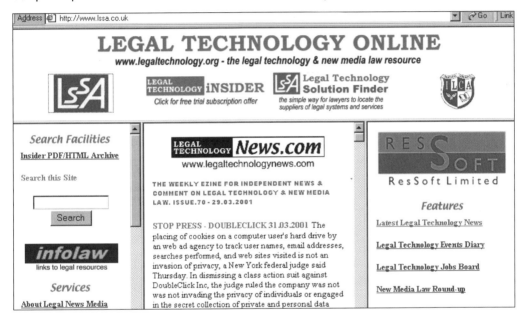

*Miles 33*
http://www.miles33.co.uk
Miles 33 is a supplier of practice and credit management systems for the legal profession. Its key product is called Precedent. The firm employs around 100 people and has offices in Bracknell, UK, and Connecticut, USA.

*MSS Management Support Systems*
http://www.mss-alphalaw.co.uk
MSS designs and supports AlphaLaw computer legal management systems, including software for case management, accounts, debt collection, debt recovery, and a child support calculator.

*PGP Awareness Project*
http://www.complaw.com/pgp.html
The site offers an introduction to the use of Pretty Good Privacy software, and related security topics, for lawyers wishing to become familiar with issues of encryption, digital signatures, and electronic commerce.

# Legal services and practice ·········································

*Pilgrim Systems*
http://www.lawsoft.co.uk
Pilgrim has served the IT needs of the legal profession since 1978. Its main product is LawSoft. Fee earners and clients can access case details and history, documents and accounting information from anywhere with internet access.

*Law.com – Practice Manager*
http://www.law.com
Based in San Francisco, Law.com sells Practice Manager, a practice management application suite, a legal tool that organises legal forms and documents through a relational database. The suite features calendaring collaboration and groupware, case management, document management and assembly, time and billing, legal cost auditing and other business-critical tools to deliver a complete virtual law office for legal professionals. It is designed for seamless integration with office products such as Microsoft Word, Microsoft Exchange, HotDocs, and Rightfax.

*Quill Computer Systems*
http://www.quill.co.uk/
Supplies legal accounting software.

*Solicitec Legal Systems*
http://www.solicitec.com
The firm's products, SolCase and SolCase Online, cover various aspects of legal practice such as debt collection, conveyancing, personal injury, criminal, and employer's liability. SolCase Online brings ecommerce to the law office, and can be used as part of an intranet, extranet or internet system to give full case management access. Clients can enquire on their cases, update existing information, record new events and create new cases.

*Solicitors Own Software*
http://www.sosbath.co.uk/
The firm produces Windows-based software for solicitors, including SOS Practice Manager.

*Thompson Moore Associates*
http://www.tma.gb.com/
Based in Bagshot, Surrey, TMA produces and supplies SiMS, the Solicitor's Integrated Management System, a comprehensive practice management system designed for the legal profession. The standard software package can be customised to specific customer requirements.

*Workrite for UK Employers*
http://www.workrite.co.uk/
The service offers workplace procedures, contracts of employment, health and safety policies, legal help line, and more.

## Legal services online

The number of legal services online in the UK is still very limited, compared for example with this fast-expanding sector in the USA, Canada and Australia. In those countries, a large number of sites are now offering general legal advice online, and numerous specialist sites cover topics such as divorce, wills and probate and conveyancing. Here are some of the best-known UK services, with one or two from other countries for comparison.

*Delia Venables – Law firms selling and marketing their services online*
http://www.venables.co.uk/selling1.htm
This is an excellent and well-maintained resource. It contains a good number of links and brief descriptions of individual firms of solicitors selling legal services directly from their web sites.

*Desktop Lawyer*
http://www.desktoplawyer.freeserve.net/law/
London-based Desktop Lawyer offers a library of Rapidocs documents prepared by UK lawyers. You can download your smart document or contract and use the service's document creation software to 'fill in the blanks'. You can then send the completed document back to FirstAssist Group's legal team for further assistance if required.

*Electronic Law Practice: An Exercise in Legal Futurology*
http://www.dur.ac.uk/Law/centre/future.html
This is an interesting discussion by Robin Widdison, Director of the Centre for Law and Computing at the University of Durham.

*Freelawyer*
http://www.freelawyer.co.uk
Freelawyer is the UK internet equivalent of a free drop-by legal centre. Its

Fig. 53. Freelawyer is an excellent example of how legal services are now being offered to consumers online.

'virtual lawyers' can provide you with an instant preliminary snapshot of the law on the particular area concerned. The legal information is provided following an interactive session in which you are asked a number of questions. You then get a tailored legal information sheet based on your replies and written in practical easy-to-understand English. It comes with a list of local specialist law firms that you can contact either directly through the site, or through your own means. This attractively-presented and efficient service could be the forerunner of many such online services.

*Instant Solicitor*
http://www.instantsolicitor.com
This service is run by Gamble Morris Hills, a firm of solicitors in the Midlands. The online service is based on the Rapidocs document assembly system. Each document is assembled by the user responding to a structured series of questions. Rapidocs analyses the answers and produces the legal document. The document centre has hundreds of documents available at discounted prices

*Law Partners*
http://www.lawpartners.com.au
A team of Australian barristers and solicitors offer online legal advice. They include specialists in wills and estate, family, immigration, and property law.

*Lawrights*
http://www.lawrights.co.uk
This is a private company set up by a team of barristers and solicitors to provide 'free, concise and independent' legal information to the public. The web site covers topics such as accident claims, adoption, children, consumer law, employment, injunctions, legal aid, private and public housing, relationships, and the Small Claims Court. In addition to documents for such matters as tenancies and wills, there are documents for agency agreements, confidentiality agreements, distribution agreements, employment contracts, internet and email usage guidelines for office workers, and even web site design agreements for developers and clients.

*Lawrite*
http://www.lawrite.co.uk
Lawrite is a UK example of the fast growing online services. It provides the latest employment law news, facts sheets on many aspects of employment law, CDs on employment law (e.g. contracts, staff handbooks, disciplinary/grievance procedures and discrimination) and other law guides.

*Legal Advice Online*
http://www.legal-advice-online.co.uk
This is a consultancy service for England and Wales with offices in Leeds, Manchester, and London. Its team of qualified solicitors and legal con-

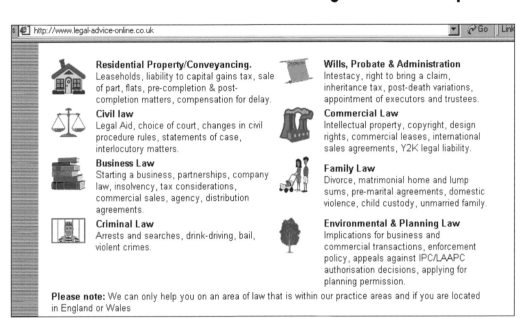

**Residential Property/Conveyancing.**
Leaseholds, liability to capital gains tax, sale of part, flats, pre-completion & post-completion matters, compensation for delay.

**Civil law**
Legal Aid, choice of court, changes in civil procedure rules, statements of case, interlocutory matters.

**Business Law**
Starting a business, partnerships, company law, insolvency, tax considerations, commercial sales, agency, distribution agreements.

**Criminal Law**
Arrests and searches, drink-driving, bail, violent crimes.

**Wills, Probate & Administration**
Intestacy, right to bring a claim, inheritance tax, post-death variations, appointment of executors and trustees.

**Commercial Law**
Intellectual property, copyright, design rights, commercial leases, international sales agreements, Y2K legal liability.

**Family Law**
Divorce, matrimonial home and lump sums, pre-marital agreements, domestic violence, child custody, unmarried family.

**Environmental & Planning Law**
Implications for business and commercial transactions, enforcement policy, appeals against IPC/LAAPC authorisation decisions, applying for planning permission.

**Please note:** We can only help you on an area of law that is within our practice areas and if you are located in England or Wales

sultants are online 24 hours a day to offer basic legal advice over the net. The basic service costs £29.99. You fill out an online submission form and they say they will respond to you by email with appropriate solutions within 24 hours of receipt of payment. Other priced services include letter writing and negotiation, express contract and document checking and drafting service, debt recovery, and various others.

Fig. 54. Legal Advice Online.

*Legalmove*
http://www.legalmove.com
This is a new service developed by the conveyancing division of Hammond Suddards Edge. It offers the public a fixed fee service with 24-hour access to details of their file, telephone support, and online updates as the matter progresses. It says it is the UK's first 'instruction to completion' online conveyancing service.

*Legal Opinion*
http://www.legalopinion.com
This is an example of an American web site where legal advice is available online through direct access to a licensed lawyer in a requested area of law and jurisdiction. The cost starts at $39.95. The publicly quoted service can provide you with access to a directory of over 7,600 lawyers who can help. With a 'two days response' promise, this service seeks to revolutionise legal advice on the web.

*Perfectly Legal*
http://www.perfectlylegal.co.uk
This London-based service offers online residential conveyancing quotes and advice. It is a division of Vizard Oldham Solicitors.

# Legal services and practice .............................................

*Which? Online – Legal Advice*
http://www.which.net/legal/contents.html
They say: 'We'll help you understand your rights as a consumer and fight for them if you have to.' The site is a service of the UK Consumer Association. You can check out the Which? Legal Service, and explore its legal archive for reports published more than two years ago.

*Wills*
http://www.wills.co.uk
Foreman Laws, a firm of solicitors in Hitchin, Hertfordshire, have developed this site where the viewer can make a will by filling in a form. The cost is from £50.

# Appendix: Searching for information

**In this appendix we will explore:**

▶ *searching the internet*
▶ *tips for searching*
▶ *bookmarking your favourite web sites*
▶ *search engines and directories*
▶ *search utilities*
▶ *portal sites for careers guidance*

. . . . . . . . . . . . . . . . . . . . . . . . . . . . . . . . . . . . . . . . . . . . . . . . . . . . . . .

## Searching the internet

The usual way to look up something on the internet is to go to the web
site of a well-known search engine or internet directory. These services
are free and open to everyone.

▶ *Search engines* – These are also known as spiders or crawlers. They
   have highly sophisticated search tools specially designed to automatically seek out web sites across the internet. They trawl through and
   index literally millions of pages of internet content. As a result they
   often find information that is not listed in the traditional internet directories.

▶ *Internet directories* – These are developed and compiled by people,
   rather than by computers. Web authors submit their web site details,
   and these details may then be listed in the relevant sections of the
   directory.

The browser that your ISP supplies you with – typically Internet Explorer
or Netscape Navigator – should include an internet seach facility, ready
for you to use, but you are perfectly free to visit any of the search engines
listed below, and use them yourself.

Most people refer to directories as search engines and lump the two
together. For the purposes of this book, we will refer to them all as
search engines. Popular search engines have now become big web
sites in their own right, usually combining many useful features. As well
as search boxes where you can type key words to summarise what you
are looking for, you will usually also find handy directories of information,
news, email and many other services. There are hundreds if not thousands of search engines freely available. The biggest and best known
are AltaVista, Excite, Google, Infoseek, Lycos and Yahoo! (the most popular of all).

## Tips for searching

1. If you want general information, try Yahoo!, Google or AltaVista first.
   For specific information, try one or more of the other search engines.
   After experimenting, many people decide on their own favourite
   search engine and stick to it most of the time.

# Searching for information......................................................

2. If you do a search for company law, the search engine will search for 'company', and search for 'law' quite separately. This could produce details of theatre companies, for example, or family law – not what you want. The way to avoid this is to enclose all your key words inside a pair of quotation marks. If you type in "company law" then only web sites with that combination of words should be listed for you.

3. George Boole was a 19th-century English mathematician who worked on logic. He gave his name to Boolean operators – simple words like AND, OR and NOT. If you include these words in your searches, it should narrow down the results, for example: "careers AND law NOT Europe". However, don't go overboard and restrict your search too much, or you may get few or no results.

4. Try out several different search engines, and see which one you like the best. Or you could obtain the handy little search utility called Web Ferret (see below): if the information is not on one search engine, Web Ferret can usually find it on one or more of the others.

## Bookmarking your favourite web sites

Your browser (usually Internet Explorer or Netscape Navigator) enables you to save the addresses of any web sites you specially like, and may want to revisit. These are called Bookmarks in Netscape, or Favorites in Internet Explorer (US spelling), and in the America Online browser. In either case, simply mouse-click on the relevant button on your browser's toolbar – Bookmarks or Favorites as the case may be. This produces a drop-down menu that you click on to add the site concerned. When you want to revisit that site later, click again on the same button; then click the name of the web site you bookmarked, and within a few seconds it should open for you.

## Search engines

*AltaVista*
http://www.altavista.com
http://www.altavista.co.uk
AltaVista is one of the most popular search sites among web users world wide. It contains details of millions of web pages on its massive and ever-growing database. You can either follow the trails of links from its home page, or (better) type in your own key words into its search box. You can even search in about 25 different languages.

*Ask Jeeves*
http://www.askjeeves.com
Ask Jeeves offers a slightly different approach to searches. It invites you to ask questions on the internet just as you would of a friend or colleague. For example you could type in something like: 'Where can I find out about environmental law?' Jeeves retrieves the information, drawing from a knowledge base of millions of standard answers.

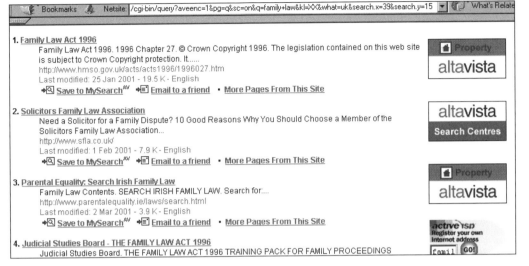

Fig. 55. Altavista being used to search for Family Law web links.

*Electronic Yellow Pages*
http://www.eyp.co.uk
These electronic yellow pages are organised on the same lines as the paper edition. Just type in the details of the information you need – anything from solicitors to courts – and it quickly searches for appropriate services in your local area.

*Excite*
http://www.excite.com
http://www.excite.co.uk
Excite is another of the top ten search engines and directories on the internet. To refine your search, simply click the check boxes next to the words you want to add and then click the Search Again button. There are separate Excite home pages for several different countries and cultures including Australia, Chinese, France, German, Italy, Japan, Netherlands, Spain, Sweden, and the USA.

*Global On-line Directory*
http://www.god.co.uk
Launched in 1996, GOD is fairly unusual among search engines in that it is UK-based, and aims to be a premier European search service. Features of the site include a 'global search' where you can search for web sites by country, state, province, county or even city by city, narrowing down the information for a more focused result.

*Google*
http://www.google.com
A new and innovative search site, popular among professional internet users, is Google, which has an easy-to-use no-nonsense format. It matches your query to the text in its index, to find relevant pages. For instance, when analysing a page for indexing, it looks at what the pages linking to that page have to say about it, so the rating partly

# Searching for information...........................................

Google™
Web Directory

Advanced Search   Preferences   Search Tips

extradition          Google Search

⦿ Search only in Law   ○ Search the Web

*Tip: In most browsers you can just hit the return key instead of clicking on the search button.*

**Law**
Society > Law                                                                     Go to Directory Home

**Categories**

Society > Law > Legal Information > International Law

Searched within the category **Law** for **extradition**.          Results **1 - 10** of about **1,170**. Search took **0.10** seconds.

Want more results? Repeat the search for **extradition** on the entire web.

ASIL Insight: Pinochet Arrest and Possible **Extradition** to ...
The Pinochet Arrest and Possible **Extradition** to Spain by Frederic L. Kirgis October
1998 On the basis of an arrest warrant issued by a judge in Spain, British ...
www.asil.org/insigh27.htm - Cached - Similar pages

   ASIL Insight: Request for **Extradition** of Miguel Cavallo
   ... Request for **Extradition** of Miguel Cavallo from Mexico to Spain for Alleged Torture

Fig. 56. Google being used to search for Extradition web links.

depends on what others say about it. This highly-regarded search facility has indexed well over a billion pages on the world wide web, and is now helping to power Yahoo! It also includes a substantial and well-categorised internet directory in which you can look things up by topic.

*HotBot*
http://hotbot.lycos.com
This is an impressive, very popular, and well-classified search engine and directory, now associated with Lycos (see below).

*Infoseek*
http://www.infoseek.co.uk
In 1994, the American 'netpreneur' Steve Kirsch founded Infoseek with the mission of helping people unleash the power of the internet. Infoseek pioneered a suite of powerful, high-quality and easy-to-use search tools. Infoseek is one of the leading search engines on the internet. This is its main UK page.

*Internet Address Finder*
http://www.iaf.net
The IAF is used by millions of web users for searching and finding the names, email addresses, and now Intel Internet videophone contacts, of other users world wide. With millions of addresses it is one of the most comprehensive email directories on the internet. By registering your email address, you will also enable others to find you.

*Internet Public Library*
http://www.ipl.org/ref/
The 'Ask-a-Question' service at the Internet Public Library is experimen-

tal. The librarians who work here are mostly volunteers with other full-time librarian jobs. Your question is received at the IPL Reference Centre and the mail is reviewed once a day and questions are forwarded to a place where all the librarians can see them and answer them. Replies are sent as soon as possible, advising whether your question has been accepted or rejected. If it has been accepted, you should receive an answer to in two to seven days.

*List of Search Engines*
http://www.search-engine-index.co.uk
This enterprising British site offers a free list of more than 800 search engines, covering all kinds of different topics. There are software search

Fig. 57. The List of Search Engines web site offers a handy guide to specialist search engines, including for law.

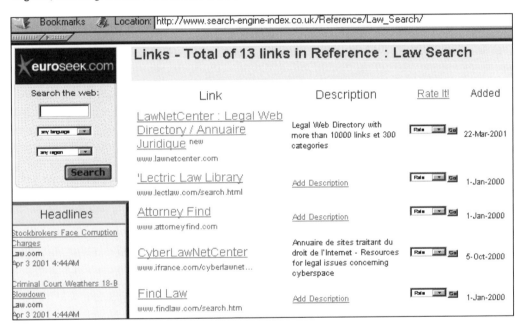

engines, multiple search engines, email/news search engines, web search engines, commercial search engines, word reference and science search, law search, TV, film and music search, image search, technology manufacturers search, and various localised search engines. For law, see:

http://www.search-engine-index.co.uk/Reference/Law.Search/

*Looksmart*
http://www.looksmart.com
This is another good directory with a huge number of catalogued sites. You can find it on the Netscape Net Search Page. If your search is not successful, you are redirected to AltaVista.

*Lycos*
http://www.lycos.com
http://www.lycos.co.uk
Lycos is another of the top ten worldwide web search engines. Lycos is

the name for a type of ground spider ('spider' being the term for a type of search engine). It searches document titles, headings, links, and keywords, and returns the first few words of each page it indexes for your search. Founded in 1995, Lycos was one of the earliest search and navigation sites designed to help people find information more easily and quickly on the world wide web. The core technology was developed at Carnegie Mellon University. Since 1997, with the media giant Bertelsmann, it has launched Lycos sites in 11 European countries.

*Metacrawler*
http://www.metacrawler.com
MetaCrawler was originally developed by Erik Selberg and Oren Etzioni at the University of Washington, and released to the internet in 1995. In response to each user query, it incorporates results from all the top search engines. It collates results, eliminates duplication, scores the results and provides the user with a list of relevant sites.

*SavvySearch*
http://www.savvysearch.com/
Owned by CNET, SavvySearch is one of the leading providers of meta-search services. Its search engine offers a single point of access to hundreds of different search engines, guides, archives, libraries, and other resources. You type in a keyword query which is then immediately sent out to all appropriate internet search engines. The results are gathered and displayed within a few seconds.

*Scoot Yahoo!*
http://scoot.yahoo.co.uk
Yahoo! has combined with the British directory Scoot to offer an excellent search facility for those looking for UK-oriented information, businesses and organisations. Once you have found the organisation you are looking for you can click straight into their web site if they have one.

*Scrub The Web*
http://www.scrubtheweb.com
Set up by a web design company, Scrub The Web has affiliations to Alta-Vista, HotBot and InfoSeek.

*Search.com*
http://search.cnet.com/
This service is run by CNET, one of the world's leading new-media companies. From the home page you can click an A-Z list of options which displays an archive of all its search engines. The list is long, but just about everything you need to master the web is there. You can search yellow pages, phone numbers, email addresses, message boards, software downloads, and easily do all kinds of special searches.

*Snap*
http://www.snap.com
Snap is by the media conglomerate NBC (National Broadcasting Cor-

poration). The site is heavily biased towards the USA. Snap is a fast, easy to use service that is becoming a significant competitor to some of the older, more established companies.

*Starting Point MetaSearch*
http://www.stpt.com/search.html
This is a powerful metasearcher that puts numerous high-quality, popular, and comprehensive search tools – general and category specific – at your fingertips.

*UK Directory*
http://www.ukdirectory.co.uk
This is a useful directory listing to UK-based web sites. You can browse it or search it. It has a well-classified subject listing. UK Directory is simple and intuitive to use. You don't need to know the name of the company, service or person to find the things you are interested in. Just look in the category that best suits your needs. It is as easy to use as a telephone directory.

*UK Plus*
http://www.ukplus.co.uk
The parent company of this UK-oriented search engine and database is Daily Mail & General Trust – owners of the *Daily Mail,* the *Mail on Sunday, London Evening Standard* and a number of UK regional newspapers – so it draws on a long publishing tradition. It has built up a big store of web site reviews written by a team of experienced journalists. Although it concentrates on UK web sites, you will also find many from all over the world which are included because it feels they could be of interest to British-based readers.

*UK Yellow Web Directory*
http://www.yell.co.uk
This site is operated by the yellow pages division of British Telecom. It is indexed 'by humans' and is searchable. A number of non-UK sites are included in the database. There is also an A to Z company listing, but note that companies whose names begin with 'The' are listed under T. A Business Compass lists 'the best' business internet resources, with links and brief descriptions.

*Webcrawler*
http://webcrawler.com
Webcrawler is a fast worker and returns an impressive list of links. It analyses the full text of documents, allowing the searcher to locate key words which may have been buried deep within a document's text. Webcrawler is now part of Excite.

*World Email Directory*
http://www.worldemail.com
This site is dedicated to email, email, more email, finding people and locating businesses and organisations. WED has access to an estimated

# Searching for information...................................................

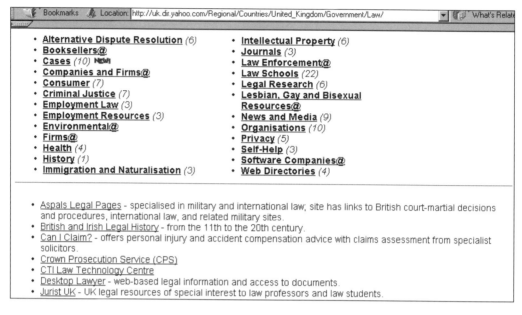

Bookmarks    Location: `http://uk.dir.yahoo.com/Regional/Countries/United_Kingdom/Government/Law/`    What's Relate

- **Alternative Dispute Resolution** *(6)*
- **Booksellers@**
- **Cases** *(10)* New
- **Companies and Firms@**
- **Consumer** *(7)*
- **Criminal Justice** *(7)*
- **Employment Law** *(3)*
- **Employment Resources** *(3)*
- **Environmental@**
- **Firms@**
- **Health** *(4)*
- **History** *(1)*
- **Immigration and Naturalisation** *(3)*

- **Intellectual Property** *(6)*
- **Journals** *(3)*
- **Law Enforcement@**
- **Law Schools** *(22)*
- **Legal Research** *(6)*
- **Lesbian, Gay and Bisexual Resources@**
- **News and Media** *(9)*
- **Organisations** *(10)*
- **Privacy** *(5)*
- **Self-Help** *(3)*
- **Software Companies@**
- **Web Directories** *(4)*

- Aspals Legal Pages - specialised in military and international law; site has links to British court-martial decisions and procedures, international law, and related military sites.
- British and Irish Legal History - from the 11th to the 20th century.
- Can I Claim? - offers personal injury and accident compensation advice with claims assessment from specialist solicitors.
- Crown Prosecution Service (CPS)
- CTI Law Technology Centre
- Desktop Lawyer - web-based legal information and access to documents.
- Jurist UK - UK legal resources of special interest to law professors and law students.

Fig. 58. The Yahoo UK Law Directory.

18 million email addresses and more than 140 million business and phone addresses worldwide. Here you'll find everything from email software, to email list servers, many worldwide email databases, business, telephone and fax directories and a powerful email search engine.

*Yahoo!*
http://www.yahoo.com
http://www.yahoo.co.uk
Yahoo! was the first substantial internet directory, and continues to be one of the best for free general searching. It contains over a billion links categorised by subject. You can 'drill down' through its well-organised categories to find what you want, or you can carry out your own searches using keywords. The site also offers world news, sport, weather, email, chat, retailing facilities, clubs, communities and many other features. Yahoo! is probably one of the search engines and directories you will use time after time, as do millions of people every day.

*Yahoo! Higher Education*
http://www.yahoo.com/Education/Higher_Education/
This search engine will give you an impressive array of links to useful HE sites.

## Search utilities

*WebFerret*
http://www.ferretsoft.com
WebFerret is an excellent little search utility. You can key in your query off-line, and when you connect it searches the web until it has collected all the references you have specified – up to 9,999 if you wish. WebFerret queries ten or more search engines simultaneously and discards any

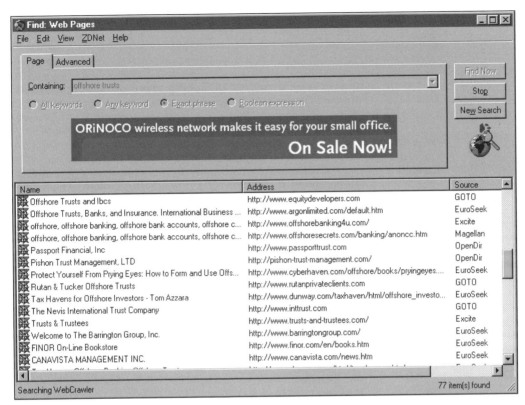

Fig. 59. Using the search utility Web Ferret to search for web pages dealing with Offshore Trusts.

duplicate results. The search engines it queries include AltaVista, Yahoo, Infoseek, Excite, and others. You can immediately visit the web pages it lists for you, even while WebFerret is still running. The trial version of the program is free, and simplicity itself. It only takes a few minutes to download from FerretSoft. Highly recommended.

## Other Internet Handbooks to help you

▶ *Exploring Yahoo! on the Internet* by David Holland. A practical guide for internet users everywhere

▶ *Getting Connected to the Internet* by Ian Hosker. A practical step-by-step guide to going online for the very first time.

▶ *Search Engines on the Internet* by Kye Valongo. A practical step-by-step guide for all internet users.

▶ *Studying Law on the Internet* by Stephen Hardy. How to use the internet for learning and study, exams and career development.

▶ *Where to Find it on the Internet* by Kye Valongo (2nd edition). Your complete guide to search engines, portals, databases, yellow pages and other internet reference tools.

# Glossary of internet terms

**access provider** – The company that provides you with access to the internet. This may be an independent provider or a large international organisation such as AOL or CompuServe. See also **internet service provider**.

**ActiveX** – A Microsoft programming language that allows effects such as animations, games and other interactive features to be included a web page.

**Adobe Acrobat** – A type of software required for reading PDF files ('portable document format'). You may need to have Adobe Acrobat Reader when downloading large text files from the internet, such as lengthy reports or chapters from books. If your computer lacks it, the web page will prompt you, and usually offer you an immediate download of the free version.

**address book** – A directory in a web browser where you can store people's email addresses. This saves having to type them out each time you want to email someone. You just click on an address whenever you want it.

**ADSL** – Asymmetric Digital Subscriber Line, a new phone line technology designed to provide an internet connection speed up to ten times faster than a typical modem.

**affiliate programme** – A system that allows you to sell other companies products via your web site.

**AltaVista** – One of the half dozen most popular internet search engines. Just type in a few key words to find what you want on the internet. See: www.altavista.com

**AOL** – America Online, the world's biggest internet service provider, with more than 27 million subscribers, and now merged with Time Warner. Because it has masses of content of its own – quite aside from the wider internet – it is sometimes referred to as an 'online' service provider rather than internet service provider. It has given away vast numbers of free CDs with the popular computer magazines to build its customer base. See: http://www.aol.com

**Apple Macintosh** – A type of computer that has its own proprietary operating system, as distinct from the MSDOS and Windows operating systems found on PCs (personal computers). The Apple Mac has long been a favourite of designers and publishers.

**applet** – An application programmed in Java that is designed to run only on a web browser. See also **Java**.

**application** – Any program, such as a word processor or spreadsheet program, designed for use on your computer.

**application service provider** A company that provides computer software via the internet, whereby the application is borrowed, rather than downloaded. You keep your data, they keep the program.

**ARPANET** – Advanced Research Projects Agency Network, an early form of the internet in 1960s America..

**ASCII** – American Standard Code for Information Interchange. It is a simple text file format that can be accessed by most word processors and text editors. It is a universal file type used for passing textual information across the internet.

**Ask Jeeves** – A popular internet search engine. Rather than just typing in a few key words for your search, you can type in a whole question or instruction, such as 'Find me everything about online investment.' It draws on a database of millions of questions and answers, and works best with fairly general questions.

**ASP** – (1) Active server page, a filename extension for a type of web page. (2) Application service provider (see above).

**attachment** – A file sent with an email message. The attached file can be anything from a word-processed document to a database, spreadsheet, graphic, or even a sound or video file. For example you could email someone birthday greetings, and attach a sound track or video clip.

**Authenticode** – Authenticode is a system where ActiveX controls can be authenticated in some way, usually by a certificate.

**avatar** – A cartoon or image used to represent someone interactively on screen.

**backup** – A second copy of a file or a set of files. Backing up data is essential if there is any risk of data loss.

**bandwidth** – The width of the electronic highway that gives you access to the internet. The higher the bandwidth, the wider this highway, and the faster the traffic can flow.

**banner ad** – This is a band of text and graphics, usually situated at the top of a web page. It acts like a title, telling the user what the content of the page is about. It invites the visitor to click on it to visit that site.

**baud rate** – The data transmission speed in a modem, measured in kps (kilobits per second).

**BBS** – Bulletin board service, a facility to read and to post public messages on a particular web site.

**binary numbers** – The numbering system used by computers. It only uses 1s and 0s to represent numbers.

**Blue Ribbon Campaign** – A widely supported campaign supporting free speech and opposing moves to censor the internet by all kinds of elected and unelected bodies. See the Electronic Frontier Foundation at: www.eff.org

**bookmark** – A file of URLs of your favourite internet sites. Bookmarks are very easily created by bookmarking (mouse-clicking) any internet page you like the look of. If you are an avid user, you could soon end up with hundreds of them! In the Internet Explorer browser and AOL they are called Favorites.

**Boolean search** – A search in which you type in words such as AND and OR to refine your search. Such words are called 'Boolean operators'. The concept is named after George Boole, a nineteenth-century English mathematician.

**bot** – Short for robot. It is used to refer to a program that will perform a task on the internet, such as carrying out a search.

**browser** – Your browser is your window to the internet, and will normally supplied by your internet service provider when you first sign up. It is the program that you use to access the world wide web, and manage your personal communications and privacy when online. By far the two most popular browsers are Netscape Communicator and its dominant rival Microsoft Internet Explorer. You can easily swap. Both can be downloaded free from their web sites and are found on the CD ROMs stuck to the computer magazines. It won't make much difference which one you use – they both do much the same thing. Opera, at http://www.opera.com is a great alternative that improves security, is faster and more efficient. America Online has its own proprietary browser which is not available separately.

**bug** – A weakness in a program or a computer system.

**bulletin board – service** – A type of computer-based news service that provides an email service and a file archive.

**cache** – A file storage area on a computer. Your web browser will normally cache (copy to your hard drive) each web page you visit. When you revisit that page on the web, you may in fact be looking at the page originally cached on your computer. To be sure you are viewing the current page, press **reload** or **refresh** on your browser toolbar. You can empty your cache from time to time, and the computer will do so automatically whenever the cache is full. In Internet Explorer, pages are saved in the Windows folder, Temporary Internet Files. In Netscape they are saved in a folder called Cache.

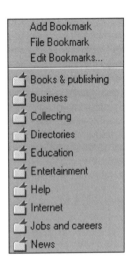

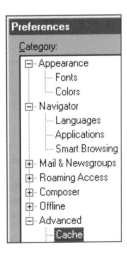

**certificate** – A computer file that securely identifies a person or organisation on the internet.

**channel (chat)** – Place where you can chat with other internet chatters. The name of a chat channel is prefixed with a hash mark, #.

**click stream** – The sequence of hyperlinks clicked by someone when using the internet.

**click through** – This is when someone clicks on a banner ad or other link, for example, and is moved from that page to the advertiser's web site.

**client** – This is the term given to the program that you use to access the internet. For example your web browser is a web client, and your email program is an email client.

**community** – The internet is often described as a net community. This refers to the fact that many people like the feeling of belonging to a group of like-minded individuals. Many big web sites have been developed along these lines, such as Yahoo!'s GeoCities and eGroups, or America Online which is strong on member services.

**compression** – Computer files can be electronically compressed, so that they can be uploaded or downloaded more quickly across the internet, saving time and money. If an image file is compressed too much, there may be a loss of quality. To read them, you uncompress 'unzip' them.

**configure** – To set up, or adjust the settings, of a computer or software program.

**content** – Articles, columns, sales messages, images, and the text of your web site.

**content services** – Web sites dedicated to a particular subject.

**cookie** – A cookie is a small text code that the server of a web page asks your browser to store on your hard drive. It may be used to store password or registration details, and pass information about your site usage to the web site concerned.

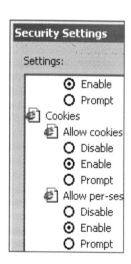

**cracker** – Someone who breaks into computer systems with the intention of causing some kind of damage or abusing the system in some way.

**crash** – What happens when a computer program malfunctions. The operating system of your PC may perform incorrectly or come to a complete stop ('freeze'), forcing you to shut down and restart.

**cross-posting** – Posting an identical message in several different newsgroups or internet mailing lists at the same time.

**cybercash** – A broad term used to describe the use of small payments made over the internet using a new form of electronic account that is loaded up with cash.

**cyberspace** – Popular term for the intangible 'place' where you go to surf – the ethereal world of computers and telecommunications on the internet.

**cybersquatting** – Using someone else's name or trademark as your domain name in the hope they will buy it from you

**cyberstalker** – An individual who pursues a victim using email, chat rooms and newsgroups.

**data** – (singular: datum). Information. Data can exist in many forms such as numbers in a spreadsheet, text in a document, or as binary numbers stored in a computer's memory.

**database** – A store of information in digital form. Many web sites make use of substantial databases to deliver maximum content at high speed to the web user.

**DHTML** – Dynamic HTML is a new web technology that enables the elements of a web page to be changed freely. DHTML allows things such as text, page styles (font colour, size etc), positioning, to be changed dynamically. Images can be made to appear and disappear, text flies around the page, and content can move around freely inside the page.

**dial up account** – This allows you to connect your computer to your internet provider's computer remotely.

**digital** – Based on the two binary digits, 1 and 0. The operation of all computers is based on this amazingly simple concept. All forms of information are capable of being digitised – numbers, words, and even sounds and images – and then transmitted over the internet.

**digital signature** – A unique personal signature specially created for use over the internet, designed to take the place of the traditional handwritten signature.

**directory** – On a PC, a folder containing your files.

**DNS** – Domain name server.

**domain name** – A name that identifies an IP (internet protocol) address. It identifies to the computers on the rest of the internet where to access particular information. Each domain has a name. For someone@somewhere.co.uk, 'somewhere' is the domain name.

**download** – Downloading means copying a file from one computer on the internet to your own computer. You do this by clicking on a button that links you to the appropriate file. Downloading is an automatic process, except that you have to click 'yes' to accept the download and give it a file name. You can download any type of file – text, graphics, sound, spreadsheet, computer programs, and so on.

**ebusiness** The broad concept of doing business to business, and business to consumer sales, over the internet.

**ecash** – Short for electronic cash. See cybercash.

**Echelon** – The name of a large governmental surveillance facility based in North Yorkshire, UK. Operated clandestinely by the US, UK and certain other governments, it is said to be eavesdropping internet traffic, using electronic dictionaries to trawl through millions of emails and other transmissions. Government surveillance everywhere is on the increase.

**ecommerce** – The various means and techniques of transacting business online.

**email** – Electronic mail, any message or file you send from your computer to another computer using your 'email client' program (such as Netscape Messenger or Microsoft Outlook).

**email address** The unique address given to you by your ISP. It can be used by others using the internet to send email messages to you. An example of a standard email address is:

my.name@virgin.net

Dial-Up Networking

**email bomb** – An attack by email in which the victim is sent hundreds or thousands of email messages in a very short period. This attack often prevents the victim receiving genuine email messages.

**emoticons** – Popular symbols used to express emotions in email, for example the well known smiley :-) which means 'I'm smiling!' Emoticons are not normally appropriate for business communications.

**encryption** – The scrambling of information to make it unreadable without a key or password. Email and any other data can now be encrypted using PGP and other freely available programs. Modern encryption has become so amazingly powerful as to be to all intents and purposes uncrackable. Law enforcers worldwide are pressing their governments for access to people's and organisation's passwords and security keys.

**Excite** – A popular internet directory and search engine used to find pages relating to specific keywords which you enter. See: www.excite.com

**ezines** – The term for magazines and newsletters published on the internet.

**FAQs** – Frequently asked questions. You will see 'FAQ' everywhere you go on the

internet. If you are ever doubtful about anything check the FAQ page, if the site has one, and you should find the answers to your queries.

**Favorites** – The rather coy term for **bookmarks** used by Internet Explorer, and by America Online. Maintaining a list of Favourites is designed to make returning to a site easier.

**file** – A file is any body of data such as a word processed document, a spreadsheet, a database file, a graphics or video file, sound file, or computer program. On a PC, a file has a filename, and filename extension showing what type of file it is.

**filtering software** – Software loaded onto a computer to prevent access by someone to unwelcome content on the internet, notably porn. The well-known 'parental controls' include CyberSitter, CyberPatrol, SurfWatch and NetNanny. They can be blunt instruments. For example, if they are programmed to reject all web pages containing the word 'virgin', you would not be able to access any web page hosted at Richard Branson's Virgin Net! Of course, there are also web sites that tell you step-by-step how to disable or bypass these filtering tools, such as: www.peacefire.org

**finger** – A tool for locating people on the internet. The most common use is to see if a person has an account at a particular internet site. Also, a chat command that returns information about the other chat user, including idle time (time since they last did anything).

**firewall** – A firewall is special security software designed to stop the flow of certain files into and out of a computer network, e.g. viruses or attacks by hackers. A firewall would be an important feature of any fully commercial web site.

**flame** – A hostile or aggressive message posted in a newsgroup or to an individual newsgroup user.

**folder** – The name for a directory on a computer. It is a place in which files are stored.

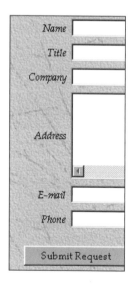

**form** – A web page that allows or requires you to enter information into fields on the page and send the information to a web site, program or individual on the web. Forms are often used for registration or sending questions and comments to web sites.

**forums** – Places for public discussion on the internet. They include Usenet newsgroups, mailing lists, and bulletin board services.

**frames** – A web design feature in which web pages are divided into several areas or panels, each containing separate information. A typical set of frames in a page includes an index frame (with navigation links), a banner frame (for a heading), and a body frame (for text matter).

**freebies** – The 'give away' products, services or other enticements offered on a web site to attract registrations.

**freespace** – An allocation of free web space by an internet service provider or other organisation, to its users or subscribers.

**Freeware** – Software programs made available without charge. Where a small charge is requested, the term is **shareware**.

**front page** – The first page of your web site that the visitor will see. FrontPage is also the name of a popular web authoring package from Microsoft.

**FTP** – File transfer protocol, the method the internet uses to speed files back and forth between computers. Your browser will automatically select this method, for instance, when you want to download your bank statements to reconcile your accounts. In practice you don't need to worry about FTP unless you are thinking about creating and publishing your own web pages: then you would need some of the freely available FTP software. Despite the name, it's reasonably easy to use.

**GIF** – Graphic interchange format. It is a widely-used compressed file format used on web pages and elsewhere to display files that contain graphic images. See also **JPEG** and **PDF**.

**Google** – A search engine and internet directory, one of the most powerful to have emerged in the last couple of years. See: www.google.com

**GUI** – Graphic user interface. It describes the user-friendly screens found in Windows and other WIMP environments (Windows, icons, mice, pointers).

**hacker** – A person interested in computer programming, operating systems, the internet and computer security. The term can be used to describe a person who breaks into computer systems with the intention of pointing out the weaknesses in a system. In common usage, the term is often wrongly used to describe crackers.

**header** – The header is that part of a message which contains information about the sender and the route that the message took through the internet.

**history list** – A record of visited web pages. Your browser probably includes a history list. It is a handy way of revisiting sites whose addresses you have forgotten to bookmark – just click on the item you want in the history list. You can normally delete all or part of the history list in your browser (but not from your ISP's records).

**hit counter** – A piece of software used by a web site to publicly display the number of hits it has received.

**hits** – The number of times the items on a web page (text, picture, link etc) have been viewed.

**home page** – The main or start page of a web site. Home sites are usually made in the form of an index and jump off page for the rest of the site.

**host** – A host is the computer where a particular file or domain is located, and from where people can retrieve it.

**HotBot** – A popular internet search engine used to find pages relating to any keywords you decide to enter.

**HTML** – Hyper text markup language, the language that a web page is usually written in. It comprises a set of tags that are used to tell the browser how to format the page. For example Hello! would tell the browser to show Hello centred on the page.

**HTTP** – Hypertext transfer protocol, the protocol used by the world wide web. It is the language spoken between your browser and the web servers. It is the standard way that HTML documents are transferred from host computer to your local browser when you're surfing the internet. You'll see this acronym at the start of every web address, for example:

http://www.abcxyz.com

With modern browsers, it is no longer necessary to enter 'http://' at the start of the address.

**hyperlink** – See **link**.

**hypertext** – This is a link on an HTML page that, when clicked with a mouse, results in a further HTML page or graphic being loaded into view on your browser.

**IANA** – The Internet Assigned Numbers Authority, the official body responsible for ensuring that the numerical coding of the internet works properly,

**ICQ** – A form of internet chat, derived from the phrase 'I seek you'. It enables users to be alerted – whenever fellow users go online, so they can have instant chat communication. The proprietary software is now owned by America Online.

**impression** – An internet advertising term that means the showing of a single instance of an advert on a single computer screen.

**Infoseek** – One of the dozen most popular internet search engines.

**Intel** – Manufacturer of the Pentium, Celeron and other microprocessors.

**internet** – The broad term for the fast-expanding network of global computers

that can access each other in seconds by phone and satellite links. If you are using a modem on your computer, you too are part of the internet. The general term 'internet' encompasses email, web pages, internet chat, newsgroups, mailing lists, bulletin boards, telnet, and – video conferencing. It is rather like the way we speak of 'the printed word' when we mean books, magazines, newspapers, newsletters, catalogues, leaflets, tickets and posters. The 'internet' does not exist in one place any more than 'the printed word' does.

**internet2** – A new form of the internet being developed for educational and academic use.

**internet account** – The account set up by your internet service provider which gives you access to the world wide web, electronic mail facilities, newsgroups and other value added services.

**internet directory** – A special web site which consists of information about other sites. The information is classified by subject area and further subdivided into smaller categories. The biggest and most widely used is Yahoo! at: www.yahoo.com – – See also **search engines**.

**Internet Explorer** – The world's most popular browser software, a product of Microsoft and leading the field against Netscape (now owned by America Online).

**internet keywords** – A commercial service that allows people to find your domain name without having to type in the other bits such as www or .com

**internet protocol (IP) number** – The numerical code that is the real domain name address of a web site.

**internet service providers** – ISPs are commercial, educational or official organisations which offer people ('users') access to the internet. The well-known commercial ones in the UK include AOL, CompuServe, BT Internet, Demon, Freeserve, NTL and Virgin Net. Commercial ISPs may levy a fixed monthly charge, though the worldwide trend is now towards free services. Services typically include access to the world wide web, email and newsgroups, as well as others such as news, chat, and entertainment. Your internet service provider will potentially know everything you do on the internet – emails sent and received, web sites visited, information downloaded, key words typed into search engines, newsgroups visited and messages read and posted. There are issues of personal privacy and data protection in this.

**Internic** – A body responsible for maintaining internet domain names. See: www.internic.net

**intranet** – Computer networking software that uses internet technology to allow communication between individuals, for example within a large commercial organisation. It often operates on a LAN (local area network).

**IP address** – An 'internet protocol' address. All computers linked to the internet have one. The address is somewhat like a telephone number, and consists of four sets of numbers separated by dots.

**IPv6** – The new internet coding system that will allow even more domain names.

**IRC** – Internet Relay Chat, an area of the internet that uses real-time transfer of text. You type a message to someone, send it, and they see it less a second or so later and then can write a reply.

**ISDN** – Integrated services digital network. This is a high-speed telephone network that can send computer data from the internet to your PC faster than a normal telephone line.

**Java** – A programming language developed by Sun Microsystems to use the special properties of the internet to create graphics and multimedia applications on web sites.

**JavaScript** – A simple programming language that can be put onto a web page to create interactive effects such as buttons that change appearance when you position the mouse over them.

Quick Click
Menu

Site Map
IRC Introduction
Newbies FAQ
IRC & Web Security

IRC Network Basics
IRC Networks
IRC Commands

mIRC Central
mIRC Installation

**JPEG** – The acronym is short for Joint Photographic Experts Group. A JPEG is a specialised file format used to display graphic files on the internet. JPEG files are smaller than similar GIF files and so have become ever more popular – even though there is sometimes a feeling that their quality is not as good as GIF format files. See also MPEG.

**key shortcut** – Two keys pressed at the same time. Usually the Control key (Ctrl), Alt key, or Shift key combined with a letter or number. For example to use Control-D, press Control, tap the D key once firmly, then take your finger off the Control key.

**keywords** – Words that sum up a web site for being indexed in search engines. For example for a cosmetic site the key words might include beauty, lipstick, make-up, fashion, cosmetic and so on.

**kick** – To eject someone from a chat channel.

**LAN** – A local area network, a computer network usually located in one building or campus.

**link** – A hypertext phrase or image that calls up another web page when you click on it. Most web sites have lots of hyperlinks, or 'links' for short. These appear on the screen as buttons, images or bits of text (often underlined) that you can click on with your mouse to jump to another site on the world wide web.

**Linux** – A new widely and freely available operating system for personal computers, and a potentially serious challenger to Microsoft. It has developed a considerable following.

**LINX** – The London Internet Exchange, the facility which maintains UK internet traffic in the UK. It allows existing individual internet service providers to exchange traffic within the UK, and improve connectivity and service for their customers.

**listserver** – An automated email system whereby subscribers are able to receive and send email from other subscribers to the list.

**log on/log off** – To access/leave a network. In the early days of computing this literally involved writing a record in a log book. You may be asked to 'log on' to certain sites and particular pages. This normally means entering your user ID in the form of a name and a password.

**lurk** – The slang term used to describe reading a newsgroup's messages without actually taking part in that newsgroup. Despite the connotations of the word, it is a perfectly respectable activity on the internet.

**macros** – 'Macro languages' are used to automate repetitive tasks in Word processors and other applications.

**mail server** – A remote computer that enables you to send and receive emails. Your internet access provider will usually provide your mail server.

**mailing list** – A forum where messages are distributed by email to the members of the forum. The two types of lists are discussion and announcement. Discussion lists allow exchange between list members. Announcement lists are one-way only and used to distribute information such as news or humour. A good place to find mailing lists is Liszt (www.liszt.com). You can normally quit a mailing list by sending an email message to request removal.

**marquee** – A moving (scrolling) line of text on a web site, used for eye-catching purposes.

**Media Player** – Microsoft Windows software on a personal computer that will play sounds and images including video clips and animations.

**metasearch engine** – A site that sends a keyword search to multiple search engines and directories so you can use many different search engines from one place.

**meta tags** – The keywords used in web page code to help search engine software rank a particular web site.

**Microsoft** – One of the world's major producers of software for personal computers, including the Windows operating systems, and the web browser Internet Explorer.

**Mixmaster** – An anonymous remailer used for security purposes. It sends and receives email messages as packages of exactly the same size and often randomly varies the delay time between receiving and remailing to make interception harder.

**modem** – This is an internal or external piece of hardware plugged into your PC. It links into a standard phone socket, thereby giving you access to the internet. The word derives from MOdulator and DEModulator.

**moderator** – A person in charge of a mailing list, newsgroup or forum. The moderator prevents unwanted messages.

**MPEG** or **MPG** – A file format used for video clips available on the internet. See also JPEG. See http://mpeg.org for further technical information

**MP3** – An immensely popular audio format that allows you to download and play music on your computer. It compresses music to create files that are small yet whose quality is almost as good as CD music. See the consumer web site: www.mp3.com –

Getting Started

My.MP3
MP3.com Mess
Store - Free Extr

Free Music

**navigate** – To click on the hyperlinks on a web site in order to move to other web pages or internet sites.

**net** – A slang term for the internet. In the same way, the world wide web is often just called the web.

**netiquette** – Popular term for the unofficial rules and language people follow to keep electronic communication in an acceptably polite form.

**Netmeeting** – A Microsoft plug-in that allows a moving video picture to be contained within a web page. It is now integrated into Windows Media Player.

**Netscape** – After Microsoft's Internet Explorer, Netscape is the most popular browser software available for surfing the internet. It has suffered in the wake of Internet Explorer, in part because of the success of Microsoft in getting the latter pre-loaded on most new PCs. Netscape Communicator comes complete with email, newsgroups, address book and bookmarks, plus a web page composer. Netscape is now owned by America Online.

**network** – Two or more computers linked together in such a way that they can communicate and exchange data.

**newbie** – Popular term for a new member of a newsgroup or internet mailing list.

**newsgroup** – A Usenet discussion group. Each newsgroup is a collection of messages, usually unedited and not checked by anyone ('unmoderated'). Messages can be placed within the newsgroup by anyone including you. It is rather like reading and sending public emails. The ever-growing newsgroups have been around for much longer than the world wide web, and are an endless source of distributed information, gossip, news, entertainment, sex, politics, resources and ideas. The 80,000-plus newsgroups are collectively referred to as Usenet, and millions of people use it every day.

**newsreader** – A type of software that enables you to search, read, post and manage messages in a newsgroup. It will normally be supplied by your internet service provider when you first sign up, or preloaded on your new computer. The best known are Microsoft Outlook, and Netscape Messenger.

**news server** – A remote computer (e.g. provided by your internet service provider) that enables you to access newsgroups. If you cannot get some or any newsgroups from your existing news server, use your favourite search engine to search for 'open news servers' – there are lots of them freely available.

**nick** – Nickname, an alias you can give yourself and use when entering a chat channel, rather than using your real name.

**Nominet** – The official body for registering domain names in the UK (for example web sites whose name ends in .co.uk).

**Notepad** – The most basic type of word processor that comes with a Windows

PC. To find it, click Start, Programs, then Accessories. Its more powerful cousin is Wordpad.

**online** – Being connected to the internet. The opposite term is offline.

**open source software** – A type of freely modifiable software, such as Linux. A definition and more information can be found at: www.opensource.org

**OS** – The operating system in a computer, for example MS DOS (Microsoft Disk Operating System), or Windows 95/98/2000.

**packet** – The term for any small piece of data sent or received over the internet on your behalf by your internet service provider, and containing your address and the recipient's address. One email message for example may be transmitted as several different packets of information, reassembled at the other end to recreate the message.

**parking** – Placing your web domain into storage until you want to use it at a later date

**password** – A word or series of letters and numbers that enables a user to access a file, computer or program. A passphrase is a password made by using more than one word.

**patch** – A small piece of software used to fix a hole or defect ('bug') in a software program.

**PC** – Personal computer, based on IBM technology. It is distinct from the Apple Macintosh which uses a different operating system

**PDA** – personal digital assistant, a mobile phone, palm top or any other handheld processor, typically used to access the internet.

**PDF** – Portable document format, a handy type of file produced using Adobe Acrobat software. It has universal applications for text and graphics.

**Pentium** – The name of a very popular microprocessor chip in personal computers, manufactured by Intel. The first Pentium IIIs were supplied with personal identifiers, which ordinary people surfing the net were unwittingly sending out, enabling user profiles to be constructed. After a storm of protest, Pentium changed the technology so that this identifier could be disabled.

**PGP** – Pretty Good Privacy, a powerful method of encoding a message before transmitting it over the internet. With PGP, a message is first compressed, then encoded with the help of keys. Just like the valuables in a locked safe, your message is safe unless a person has access to the right keys.

**ping** – You can use a ping test to check the connection speed between your computer and another computer.

**plug-in** – An additional program that will allow you to enhance the effects that your browser can display. Macromedia Shockwave is a well-known plugiin.

**PoP** – Point of presence. This refers to the dial-up phone numbers available from your ISP. If your ISP does not have a local point of presence (i.e. local access phone number), then don't sign up – your telephone bill will rocket because you will be charged national phone rates. All the major ISPs have local numbers covering the whole of the country.

**portal site** – Portal means gateway. Portals are web sites with hundreds or even thousands of links, which you use as a jumping off point to explore the internet. Yahoo! is a good example of a general portal site: www.yahoo.com

**post** – The common term used for sending ('posting') messages to a newsgroup. Posting messages is very like sending emails, except of course that they are public and everyone can read them. Also, newsgroup postings are archived, and can be read by anyone in the world years later. Because of this, many people feel more comfortable using an alias (made-up name) when posting messages.

**privacy** – Unless you take steps to protect yourself, you have practically no personal privacy online. Almost all your activity online can be electronically logged, analysed and archived by internet organisations, government agen-

cies, police and other surveillance services. You are also leaving a permanent trail of data on your computer. But then, if you have nothing to hide you have nothing to fear, or do you? To explore privacy issues worldwide visit the authoritative Electronic Frontier Foundation web site (www.eff.org) and for the UK: www.netfreedom.org

**program** – A series of coded instructions designed to automatically control a computer in carrying out a specific task. Programs are written in special languages including Java, JavaScript, VBScript, and ActiveX.

**protocol** – A set of rules that lets computers agree how to communicate. FTP (file transfer protocol) is how computers communicate when transmitting files, and HTTP (hypertext transfer protocol) is the protocol used when your browser fetches all of the components of a web page.

**proxy** – An intermediate computer or server, used for reasons of security.

**Quicktime** – A popular free software program from Apple Computers. It is designed to play sounds and images including video clips and animations on both Apple Macs and personal computers.

**QuickTime™**

**radio button** – A button that, when clicked, looks like this: ◉

**refresh, reload** – The refresh or reload button on your browser toolbar tells the web page you are looking at to reload to ensure you are viewing the latest version.

**register** – You may have to give your name, personal details and financial information to some sites before you can continue to use the pages. Site owners may want to produce a mailing list to offer you products and services. Registration is also used to discourage casual traffic.

**registered user** – Someone who has filled out an online form and then been granted permission to access a restricted area of a web site. Access is usually obtained by logging on, in other words entering a password and user name.

**remailer** – A remailer preserves your privacy by acting as a go-between when you browse or send email messages. An anonymous remailer is simply a computer connected to the internet that can forward an email message to other people after stripping off the header of the messages. Once a message is routed through an anonymous remailer, the recipient of that message, or anyone intercepting it, can no longer identify its origin.

**RFC** – Request for comment. RFCs are the way that the internet developers publicly propose changes and discuss standards and procedures.

**RIP** – The Regulation of Investigatory Powers Act, a controversial UK law passed in 2000 which enables the police to carry out secret surveillance of internet users, using so-called 'black boxes' installed at internet service providers.

**RSA** – One of the most popular methods of encryption, and used in Netscape browsers. See: www.rsa.com

**router** – A machine that directs internet data (network packets) from one internet location to another.

**rules** – The term for message filters in Outlook Express.

**script** – A script is a set of commands written into the HTML tags of a web page. Script languages such as JavaScript and VBScript work in a similar way to macros in a word processor. Scripts are hidden from view but are executed when you open a page or click a link containing script instructions.

**scroll, scroll bar** – To scroll means to move part of a page or document into view or out of view on the screen. Scrolling is done by using a scroll bar activated by the mouse pointer. Grey scroll bars automatically appear on the right and/or lower edge of the screen if the page contents are too big to fit into view.

**search engine** – A search engine is a web site you can use for finding something on the internet. The technology variously involves the use of 'bots' (search robots), spiders or crawlers. Popular search engines have developed into big web sites and information centres in their own right. There are hundreds of them. Among the best known are AltaVista, Excite, Google, Infoseek , Lycos, Metasearch and Webcrawler. See also **internet directories**.

**secure servers** – The hardware and software provided so that people can use their credit cards and leave other details without the risk of others seeing them online. Your browser will tell you when you are entering a secure site.

**secure sockets layer (SSL)** – Special technology which ensures secure financial transactions and data flow over the internet.

**security certificate** – Information that is used by the SSL protocol to establish a secure connection. A security certificate contains information about who it belongs to, who it was issued by, some form of unique identification, valid dates, and an encrypted fingerprint that can be used to verify the contents of the certificate.

**server** – Any computer on a network that provides access and serves information to other computers.

**shareware** – Software that you can try before you buy. Usually there is some kind of limitation such as an expiry date. To get the registered version, you must pay for the software, typically $20 to $40. A vast amount of shareware is now available on the internet.

**Shockwave** – A popular piece of software produced by Macromedia, which enables you to view animations and other special effects on web sites. You can download it free and in a few minutes from Macromedia's web site. The effects can be fun, but they slow down the speed at which the pages load into your browser window.

**signature file** – This is a little text file in which you can place your address details, for adding to email and newsgroup messages. Once you have created a signature file, it is appended automatically to your emails. You can of course delete or edit it.

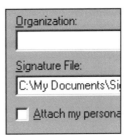

**Slashdot** – One of the leading technology news web sites, found at: http:// slashdot.org

**smiley** – A form of **emoticon**.

**snail mail** – The popular term for the standard postal service involving post-persons, vans, trains, planes, sacks and sorting offices.

**sniffer** – A program on a computer system designed to collect information. Sniffers are often used by crackers to harvest passwords and user names, and by surveillance agencies to target possible wrong doers.

**spam** – The popular term for electronic junk mail – unsolicited and unwelcome email messages sent across the internet. There are various forms of spam-busting software which you can now obtain to filter out unwanted email messages.

**SSL** – Secure socket layer, a key part of internet security technology.

**subscribe** – The term for accessing a newsgroup or email list in order to read and post – messages in the group. There is no charge, and you can subscribe, unsubscribe and resubscribe at will with a click of your mouse. Unless you post a message, no-one in the group will know that you have subscribed or unsubscribed.

**surfing** – Slang term for browsing the internet, especially following trails of links on pages across the world wide web.

**sysop** – Systems operator, someone rather like a moderator for example of a chat room or bulletin board service.

**TCP/IP** – Transmission control protocol/internet protocol, the essential technology of the internet.

**telnet** – Software that allows you to connect via the internet to a remote computer and work as if you were a terminal linked to that system.

**theme** – A term in web page design. A theme describes the general colours and graphics used within a web site. Many themes are available in the form of

# Glossary of internet terms ........................................

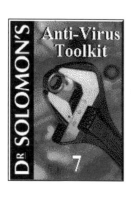

readymade templates.

**thread** – An ongoing topic in a Usenet newsgroup or mailing list discussion. The term refers to the original message on a particular topic, and all the replies and other messages which spin off from it. With news reading software, you can easily 'view thread' and thus read the related messages in a convenient batch.

**thumbnail** – A small version of a graphic file which, when clicked, displays to a larger version.

**top level domain** – The last code in the domain name, such as .com or .uk

**traceroute** – A program that traces the route from your machine to a remote system. It is useful if you need to discover a person's ISP, for example in the case of a spammer.

**traffic** – The amount of data flowing across the internet, to a particular web site, newsgroup or chat room, or as emails.

**trojan horse** – A program that seems to perform a useful task but is really a malevolent program designed to cause damage to a computer system.

**UNIX** – This is a computer operating system that has been in use for many years, and still is used in many larger systems. Most ISPs use it.

**uploading** – The act of copying files from your PC to a server or other PC on the internet, for example when you are publishing your own web pages. The term is most commonly used to describe the act of copying HTML pages onto the internet via FTP.

**URL** – Uniform resource locator, the address of each internet page. For instance the URL of Internet Handbooks is http://www.internet-handbooks.co.uk

**Usenet** – The collection of well over 80,000 active newsgroups that make up a substantial part of the internet.

**virtual reality** – The presentation of a lifelike scenario in electronic form. It can be used for gaming, business or educational purposes.

**virtual server** – A portion of a PC that is used to host your own web domain (if you have one).

**virus** – A computer program maliciously designed to cause havoc to people's computer files. Viruses can typically be received when downloading program files from the internet, or from copying material from infected disks. Even Word files can now be infected. You can protect yourself from the vast majority of them by installing some inexpensive anti-virus software, such as Norton, McAfee or Dr Solomon.

**WAP** – Wireless application protocol, new technology that enables mobile phones to access the internet.

**web** – Short for the world wide web. See **WWW** below.

**web authoring** – Creating HTML pages to upload onto the internet. You will be a web author if you create your own home page for uploading onto the internet.

**web-based chat** – A form of internet chat which is conducted just using web pages, and not requiring special software like IRC and ICQ. For web-based chat, your browser must be Java-enabled. Most modern browsers are Java-enabled by default.

**web client** – Another term for a browser.

**Webcrawler** – A popular internet search engine used to find pages relating to specific keywords entered.

**webmaster** – Any person who manages a web site.

**web page** – Any single page of information you can view on the world wide web. A typical web page includes a unique URL (address), headings, text, images, and hyperlinks (usually in the form of graphic icons, or underlined text). One web page usually contains links to lots of other web pages, either within the same web site or elsewhere on the world wide web.

**web ring** – A network of interlinked web sites that share a common interest.

**web site** – A set of web pages, owned or managed by the same person or orga-

138

nisation, and which are interconnected by hyperlinks.

**whois** – A network service that allows you to consult a database containing information about someone. A whois query can, for example, help to find the identity of someone who is sending you unwanted email messages.

**Windows** – The ubiquitous operating system for personal computers developed by Bill Gates and the Microsoft Corporation. The Windows 3.1 version was followed by Windows 95, further enhanced by Windows 98 and Windows 2000.

**wizard** – A feature of many software programs that guides you through its main stages, for example with the use of readymade templates.

**WWW** – The world wide web. Since it began in 1994 this has become the most popular part of the internet. The web is now made up of more than a billion web pages of every imaginable description, typically linking to other pages. Based on a concept of the British computer scientist, Tim Berners-Lee, its growth has been exponential and looks set to continue so.

**WYSIWYG** – 'What you see is what you get.' If you see it on the screen, then it should look just the same when you print it out.

**Yahoo!** – The world's most popular internet directory and search engine, and valued on Wall Street at billions of dollars: www.yahoo.com

**zip/unzip** – Many files that you download from the internet will be in compressed format, especially if they are large files. This is to make them quicker to download. These files are said to be zipped or compressed. Unzipping these compressed files means returning them to their original size ready for use. Zip files have the extension '.zip' and are created (and unzipped) using WinZip or a similar popular software package.

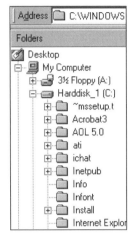

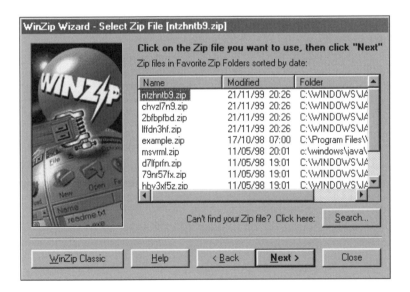

# Index

# Index...........................................................